WHAT O

ABOUT *DISCOVER YOUR GREAT ADVENTURE*

"Nancy Beverly is a marvelous writer who will sweep you into places and adventures both exotic and familiar. You'll not only be delightfully entertained, but each one will also equip you for whatever journey God has next for you. Open this book, grab the ticket, and go!"
— Leslie Leyland Fields, international speaker, multi-award-winning writer of 14 books, including *Nearing a Far God: Praying the Psalms With our Whole Selves*

"Nancy Beverly has done it again! If you want to look at life differently and courageously experience the adventure of living in God's purposes, *Discover Your Great Adventure* is for you. Her entertaining experiences provide insight, humor, and a roadmap that continually points you to Christ. A must for life's journey."
— Tez Brooks, writing coach, editor, and award-winning author of *Debriefing: Meditations for Those Who Protect and Serve*

"What's better than stories well told? Adventures for God well-lived. In *Adventures*, you'll get both. You'll laugh, reflect, and gain courage to follow God into your own adventures. A wonderful read about one person's following-God life that will be sure to inspire. I highly recommend it!"
— Lori Roeleveld, multi-award-winning author of six books, including *Graceful Influence*; owner of Take Heart! coaching and freelance

"Nancy Beverly is a masterful storyteller! Nancy reveals how God transformed her from a frightened young girl who always played it safe and never accepted challenges beyond her control, to a woman who lives on the frontlines where God is changing lives through her. The reflect and consider sections at the end of each chapter offer an opportunity to ponder what part of the compelling story most impacted you."
— Gail Porter, award-winning author of *Will the Real Person Please Stand Up; Free to be the Real You;* and *Living on the Path of Freedom*

"Do you want a book that will keep you devouring chapter after chapter and not want to stop? Read *Discover Your Great Adventure.* Kidnapping, earthquakes, scary rides, a mysterious tea leaf bungler, and a love affair—this book has it all. Who knows, maybe as you read Nancy's stories, new adventures will appear on your horizon. Grab a copy and lay hold of fresh inspiration and courage to fully live. "
— Tanya Onu, coordinator of Global Church Movement Prayer Initiative, Eastern Europe

"Nancy is one of the most whimsical people I know, with a curiosity about life and people. Not only does she keep me laughing, but she challenges me to seek opportunities to let go of my own fears and trust God each step of my life."
— Maggie Bruehl, writing coach and editor, award-winning author of *Suspended: Living with Dying* and *Splash: Captured Moments in Time*

"Nancy's stories take us on international adventures—each one unique and captivating! Her raw honesty unveils so many unexpected paths that God has taken her on. By stepping out of their comfort zone, Nancy and her husband Peter have been blessed by following a loving and unchanging God."
— Richard Ward, global entrepreneur and traveler to 88 countries

"After living overseas in the same apartment building as Nancy, I can say her stories are just like her: full of joy, curiosity, laughter, and a contagious love for the Lord. That same spark shines through every page of this book. Like Nancy herself, these stories carry a quiet depth that gently points us back to the Lord.
I read the whole thing in one sitting and didn't want to put it down! Easy to read, inspiring, and delightfully engaging, this book is a joy-filled journey you won't want to miss!"
— Kirsten Mount, founder of Creative Prayer Collaborative

"Through reading this book, you have the opportunity to taste and experience what it means to be "fully alive" as a human being by risking trusting Jesus in those places of feeling helpless and weak. His strength is made perfect in weakness. Living "alive" is our greatest adventure!"
— Roger Shepherd MA. MA. LMHC, president of Florida Counseling Foundation

NANCY BEVERLY

Discover Your Great Adventure

ONE ORDINARY LIFE. ONE EXTRAORDINARY GOD.

ONE INCREDIBLE ADVENTURE!

Published by Bright Road Publishers.

Cover photo taken by Nancy Beverly, Jiuzhaigou National Park, Sichuan Province, China.
Photos inside of this book were taken by Nancy Beverly.
Cover and design by Collin Smith Creative (collinsmithcreative.com).
Printed in the United States of America.

The names of some people and locations have been changed or omitted to protect the identities of individuals and mission work involved.

Dedicated to my dearly loved grandchildren
Ava, Blake, Beckham, Austin, Curren, Anderson, and Brooks.

And to those who open this book
searching for something more.

With prayers that you discover the One who created you for incredible adventures!

"As you love God and serve Him, you will undoubtedly experience the greatest adventure life has to offer."

Dr. Bill Bright,
founder of Campus Crusade for Christ, Int.

Table of Contents

Cocoon Breaker

Whizzing to the airport
Alone
*In the back of an open-ended songthaew**
Nonchalantly
Holding my luggage with one foot
To keep it from flying out the back,
Bracing myself with the other foot
To keep me from flying out the back.

No doors or glass obscure my view.
Nothing protects me.
The panorama through wide-open windows
Intoxicates my senses.

Gilded spirit houses and winged idols,
Tributes to the king,
Blur past me
As I one-handedly eat Kentucky Fried Chicken.
I keep the other hand free
To grab the overhead bar for sudden stops.

The strong fumes don't alarm me.
Am I sitting above a leaky exhaust pipe?

I have become someone I don't recognize.
When did this life become normal
For an overly cautious, small-town girl?

When the Lord of the universe expanded my heart
He expanded my world —
Inviting me out of my safe cocoon,
To charge into what He created me for.

Risk and love of adventure had been trapped inside,
Waiting for Him to unlock the door.

**songthaew- a type of passenger truck in Thailand*

PREFACE

ADVENTURE, ANYONE?

True confession: I am an unlikely adventurer.

Maybe you are, too.

This book is for anyone who longs for a meaningful, interesting life, but you may not know where to begin.

What is adventure?

For each person, it looks different. Adventure is doing anything outside your comfort zone. It's trying something new, taking a step of faith.

Maybe you would take that new job you're not sure would be better than the one left behind. Or accept a party invitation when you're not confident meeting new people. Adventure involves the uncomfortable choices you must take to overcome whatever keeps you stuck in a smaller universe than you prefer.

Why do we need adventure? It's the spice of life, the difference between humdrum and magnificent. Like plain tofu that's transformed when a gourmet chef stirs in his secret ingredients.

If I had stayed in my small, familiar world, I would have missed out on so much! Joining your life with something—or someone—bigger than yourself expands your world, inside and out. Adventure keeps you feeling young because you are always learning something new.

The adventures in the pages ahead range from childhood to ten years overseas to the present. You will discover that if *I* can become an adventurer, *anyone* can become one. The most crucial ingredient is… well, read on.

I hope you laugh, cry, and see yourself in my stories. I hope they motivate you to pursue your unique adventure. The road ahead won't always be smooth and predictable, but your life will seldom be boring!

I pray that reading about my escapades will encourage you to take that first step into whatever is calling you. You don't have to travel the world like I did.

Your incredible adventure might be in your own backyard.

SECTION ONE

Find a Solid Foundation

I looked out at this busy intersection from our sixth-floor balcony in East Asia every day for almost ten years. We enjoyed a broad assortment of interesting sights, but this was my favorite. I shook my head as I evaluated this acrobatic feat, amazed by how one man cupped the bottom of the ladder in his hands while the other one climbed to the top.

How is the ladder holding his weight just by leaning on the wires? These two workers seemed to defy the laws of gravity. The man at the bottom lost his helmet somewhere in the shuffle, so this arrangement is not safe for him either.

They demonstrated a lack of the first essential ingredient needed to discover your great adventure: a solid, dependable foundation.

CHAPTER 1

KIDNAPPED!

Did that rickshaw driver just race away with my ten-year-old daughter?

I stood there, paralyzed by disbelief, as the motor-powered vehicle vanished from my sight. I was still trying to process what happened when my quick-thinking son, Andrew, dropped his grocery bags and flew like a bullet after them.

The ordeal began as an ordinary grocery trip during our college-age son's visit to our home in East Asia. We carried our bags out of the store and found a rickshaw driver waiting at the curb.

After my daughter climbed into the rickshaw, the driver motioned for Andrew and me to step aside. Thinking she wanted to pull closer to the curb, we moved back. But instead of coming closer, she revved up the gas and disappeared down the street, taking my precious child with her.

Andrew caught up with the speeding vehicle, grabbed onto the back, and dug his heels into the asphalt so hard that the rickshaw slowed down. When the woman turned around to discover why her motorbike had decelerated, he ran to the front and started pulling on the handlebar, shouting "Stop! Stop!"

As the driver tried to push Andrew off, my daughter jumped out.

Still grasping her grocery bag, she was pretty shaken up. I was, too! But thankfully, she was safe. *She was safe!* From then on, we had an adult enter vehicles before she did.

What was that woman doing? Was she trying to kidnap my daughter? Or did something frighten her and she just took off? We will never know for sure, but God still had us covered.

What would I have done if Andrew hadn't been visiting and had not come along shopping? What would have happened to our little girl? But Andrew *was* with us. I was incredibly grateful and amazed he acted so quickly, risking his life for his sister. God orchestrated events precisely the way that was needed.

Not everyone has a big brother to rescue them from harm, and not every story ends well. God doesn't promise we won't encounter evil in this world, but we have His unchanging promise He will be our shield and protector in the midst of trouble. I believe when we get to heaven, we will realize there were many close calls from which we were protected and many bad things could have been worse.

Reflect:

On a scale of 1 to 10, how much does fear concerning your physical safety keep you from trying new things? Consider why that number isn't lower. What might help you decrease it by 1 or 2?

Consider:

"The LORD is my rock, my fortress, and my savior; my God is my rock, in whom I find protection. He is my shield, the power that saves me, and my place of safety."

— Psalm 18:2 NLT

How could this verse help you to move forward with an adventure you believe God wants you to pursue?

CHAPTER 2

Indoor Earthquake

Explosions like machine gun fire jolted me out of my Christmas morning slumber into high alert. Adrenaline surged as I rushed to the living room doorway, where my husband Peter's shouts joined the uproar.

Were our Christmas tree lights exploding?

We watched in amazement. Our ceramic floor tiles rippled like dominoes—cracking, rising, and falling. Finally, all was quiet.

Oh, not this again.

The heat of our East Asia apartment had collided with the cold air from the unheated apartment below, expanding and cracking the tiles. The floor surrounding our tree resembled a topographical map of Rocky Mountain National Park.

I was terrified the first time this happened three years earlier. I had no idea what lay underneath the tiles and I imagined two-by-four beams with gaping holes opening to the floor below. One wrong move and... hello, neighbor!

When the repairman glued the cracked tiles down, he showed us the solid concrete beneath them. We felt relieved when we realized the tiles were cosmetic and did not affect the structure.

This time, it still unnerved me to step on a tile and feel it move and crackle, but the fear was gone. There was a solid foundation. No matter how rickety the floor appeared, there was something substantial underneath. Knowing the concrete lay underneath made all the difference.

Peter maneuvered across the ceramic tile mountains to retrieve our stranded Christmas presents. Our holiday festivities began as usual, and the repairman glued the tiles down the next day.

Isn't this like walking with Jesus? Life shifts and shakes and sounds scary, and sometimes we imagine a deep hole into which we may stumble. But Jesus is stronger than concrete and two-by-fours. No matter what buckles beneath us, no matter how precarious the path before us seems, He will always hold us up. We can confidently move forward knowing that whatever unknowns we encounter, what is beneath us will remain the same.

No one and nothing is solid except the unchangeable foundation Himself, God. We can stand on that!

Reflect:

What factors do you wish were more certain and predictable in your life?

Consider:

"Therefore everyone who hears these words of mine and puts them into practice is like a wise man who built his house on the rock. The rain came down, the streams rose, and the winds blew and beat against that house; yet it did not fall, because it had its foundation on the rock."

— *Matthew 7:24-25 NIV*

Do you spend time reading and applying Bible truths on a regular basis? How could you build the stability of God's Word into your life more?

CHAPTER 3

Internet Repair

We excitedly imagined how fast our internet would be as they replaced our old wires with the latest fiber-optic cable. But just as we were testing it later that day, poof!

Disconnected.

Restarting the modem several times made no difference. We called the company, and they came later the next morning and repaired it. Sitting in front of our laptops that evening, our plans to catch up on emails were thwarted by another sudden service disruption.

They fixed it again. Then, the same thing happened a third time. The connection worked fine during the day, but in the early evening, it suddenly disconnected. The mystery deepened.

Fortunately, the third time the repairmen came, a friend who speaks the language very well was visiting and asked them to explain the problem. They led her down to the internet cable box in the stairwell on the first floor.

The workers showed her the box held seven spaces for seven internet cables. There were now eight wires from eight apartments, but only seven cable spaces. When the workers installed ours, they unplugged another apartment's cable to plug in ours. This set up a type of musical chairs between apartments. Since the cable box lay unlocked and open, when that person came home from work each day, he unplugged our cable and inserted his wire again.

"Did you consider installing a bigger box with more cable connections?" our friend asked. They said they would have to get their boss's permission, which wouldn't be easy.

"Did you think of closing and locking the box so people can't mess with the cables?" she inquired.

They took her suggestion, and from that time on our internet worked without fail.

In life, it is easy to "switch the internet wires" and never deal with the root of a problem. What foundational beliefs determine how I look at life? Why is it hard for me to step out of the ordinary? Why am I afraid of failure in one area but bravely jump into other challenges? I could exhaust myself trying to control outward circumstances without taking time to discover what root issue gives them power.

Jesus can gently uncover and heal emotional wounds and the lies hiding underneath, freeing us to venture into new areas of growth and exploration. This inner discovery and healing process is an adventure in itself.

Reflect:

What root issue may keep you from stepping out of your comfort zone? What could you do today to begin to identify it and explore how to loosen its grip?

Consider:

"Search me, O God, and know my heart; test me and know my anxious thoughts. Point out anything in me that offends you and lead me along the path of everlasting life."

— Psalms 139:23,24 NLT

If you are able to pray it from the heart, pray these verses above as your own prayer to God.

CHAPTER 4

THE TREASURE THAT CANNOT BE STOLEN

Sixty seconds of distraction… and one of my most valued possessions was gone. Peter and I were halfway down the airport ramp when I remembered I had tucked my camera bag under the seat. Peter hurried back, but it was too late.

My camera was stolen.

I had saved up for this special camera for more than a year. My daughter and I had so much fun with its creative features, but now my treasure was gone.

As we rode home from the airport, tears rolled down my face. Several condemning thoughts bounced around in my mind. *You are overreacting! Get control of yourself. Why did you put it under your seat in the first place? Why were you so careless?*

I angrily thought about who stole my bag, assuming it was the man who sat in front of me.

Suddenly, a gentle melody interrupted my mind's cacophony of voices.

"Lord, you are more precious than silver;
Lord, you are more costly than gold;
Lord, you are more beautiful than diamonds;
and nothing I desire compares with You."[1]

It was as if Jesus asked me, "Am I not more precious than a digital camera? Am I more beautiful than the photos you lost? How does your desire for Me compare with your desire for these items?"

I'd like to say I praised God from the start, but I didn't. He patiently led me through my sadness and anger as I poured it out to Him. Then, I was able to respond. *Yes, Lord! Absolutely! You are worth infinitely more! I will really miss my camera, but if losing it will somehow draw me closer to You, You are worth it!*

I drifted off to sleep that evening, peacefully surrounded by the comforting truth that knowing Him is certainly more precious than anything or anyone else. There is nothing and no one who can ever steal His Presence from you or me.

A thought interrupted my sleep that night. It was so fleeting that I didn't remember it until three days later. *Doesn't the credit card I used to buy the camera have a refund guarantee if something purchased is stolen?* I excitedly hunted for the fine print on my credit card account.

Yes! It was true! I could be refunded for anything bought on that credit card if the item was reported as stolen within 90 days of purchase. I frantically rummaged through our receipts to find the purchase date, my heart pounding as I held my breath, hoping it was within the required time limit. My camera had been purchased 88 days earlier, squeaking through before the 90-day deadline! Someone once said, "God is never in a hurry, but He's never late." This was one of those occasions.

I was filled with awe at God's goodness as I gathered the paperwork

---

1 DeShazo, Lynn. "More Precious Than Silver." Integrity's Hosanna! Music, 1992 ***More Precious than Silver** © **Copyright** 1982, Arr. © 1992 Integrity›s Hosanna! Music, c/o Integrity Music, Inc., P.O. Box 16813, Mobile, AL 36616. © **Copyright** 1982, Arr. © 1992 Integrity›s Hosanna!

for my refund and soon held a replacement for the stolen one. I was sad to lose the pictures on my original camera, but in their place, I received a picture with far more value: a closer glimpse of the goodness and compassion of my God.

Reflect:
What do you consider to be your most valuable possession? Why?

Consider:
"...I count all things as loss in view of the surpassing value of knowing Christ Jesus my Lord, for whom I have suffered the loss of all things, and count them but rubbish in order that I may gain Christ..."

— Phil. 3:8 NASB

Why do you think Paul considered knowing Jesus to be more valuable than anything else?

CHAPTER 5

YOUR ADVENTURE OR MINE?

When is the enjoyable part of this journey going to start?

Our fragile kayaks approached an outcropping of jagged rocks as the waves angrily splashed around us.

Nestled in the middle of the Andaman Sea, about a two-hour boat ride from Southern Thailand, Koh Ngai is a great place to get away from it all. I mean, far away from it all. There are no roads, stores, or medical facilities. There is a short strip of beach with one hotel, one restaurant, and a couple of small huts for the workers.

The rest of the island is a beautiful primitive jungle, with a small sandy inlet on the isolated backside where waves deposit an inordinate amount of sea glass. When waves repeatedly slam together sand and pieces of broken glass, what remains are delicately smooth multicolored pieces of iridescent glass. My friend, Shelly, had found bucketsful on previous visits to that cove.

Paddling in the ocean was not on my bucket list, but Shelly's enthusiasm made her invitation irresistible. Shelly was convinced we would find enough sea glass to make it worth the effort to get there. When she invited our twelve-year-old daughters to join us, I assumed she knew it would be a fun mother-daughter outing. But I was beginning to think that my idea of safe was not the same as Shelly's.

We churned through the waters that swirled around the boulders. Our kayaks popped and gurgled, then barely glided over the rocks below into the vast, desolate sea.

The four of us stared at the endless ocean stretching around us. When we passed through the rough waves into the uncivilized backside of this island, we lost cellphone connection with family and friends back at the resort.

As our kayaks grew closer to the coveted sea glass with each stroke, I noticed we were not alone. A small, motorized fishing boat was anchored close to our destination. Looking in all directions to assess our level of safety, my stomach tightened. We were four females in two human-powered vessels, meeting a boat with a motor. *How many are on the ship? Are they friendly? Will we disturb them? More importantly, will they disturb us?*

With no signs of life as we passed the vessel, we dragged our kayaks onto the sandy inlet and tackled the harvesting of our treasure. At that point, I couldn't have cared less about sea glass. My eyes were riveted on that boat, watching for signs of life. Then I noticed something that made my heart pound in my chest.

Two black flags with ominous-looking symbols hung from their mast.

"What does a black flag mean?" I stuttered nervously. Knowing we were close to radical Islamist territory, I knew it couldn't be good. My imagination ran wild, and I assessed whether we could escape into the jungle behind us.

"I don't know, probably just hanging their laundry," Shelly replied distractedly, intent on her jewels in the sand. But these were not t-shirts waving in the wind!

I prayed hard for God's protection until my friend filled her bucket. Then, leaving a wide distance between the boat and our kayaks, I breathed slowly as we ever-so-quietly slipped past. A pair of tanned bare feet stuck out from underneath a canvas at the end of the boat.

Our potential captor slept while we escaped.

Checking the internet back in our hotel, I found three possible meanings for this black flag: pirates, followers of Mohammed, or anarchists. It can also mean they will kill anyone captured rather than take them prisoner. None of these options sounded like the kind of people we wanted to meet.

I honestly am not sure what happened to the sea glass I collected. It wasn't worth the trouble. My greatest treasures were the insights I learned about God and myself.

The level of risk my friend was comfortable with was different from mine. God would not abandon me just because I went to a deserted beach where I encountered potential extremes. But He also didn't expect me to blindly follow someone else's adventure. He wanted me to be sure it was what He called me to do.

God is the only one we should follow.

But if He leads you outside of your familiar world and you are caught in a dangerous situation beyond your control, remember He can protect you from anarchist pirates known to leave no survivors.

Reflect:

What dream are you following? Is it yours or someone else's?

Consider:

"When Peter saw him, he said, 'Lord, what about him?' Jesus told him, 'If it's my will for him to remain until I come back, how does that concern you? You must keep following me!'"

—John 21:21,22 ISV

What step of faith is God calling you to take today that is separate from anyone else's path of faith?

CHAPTER 6

A Scary Ride

How quickly can I shove open the car door and roll out when he slows down on a curve? Would Peter be able to escape also?

I stared out the back seat window as skyscrapers gave way to smaller buildings and then to fields of tall weeds. The lump in my stomach grew. I kicked Peter's foot next to me and gave him a glance that silently shouted, *Where are they taking us? What should we do?* My eyes begged him for an answer, but he had none.

A few weeks earlier, a friendly young local woman on the bus struck up a conversation with Peter. Americans held instant celebrity status, and locals often wanted to practice their English. Peter did what he always did with friendly women who wanted to practice English: he gave her my phone number.

She and I texted a few times, and she invited Peter and me to dinner. She and her boyfriend offered us a ride to her home, which she explained was "downtown."

So, we did what we had warned our children not to do: we took a ride from strangers to a place we didn't know. Her boyfriend spoke no English and hers was limited, but they were friendly. However, I grew increasingly uncomfortable when I noticed we were heading in the opposite direction of downtown.

"So… your apartment is downtown, and that's where we're headed?" I asked her.

"Yes," she assured me as we drove toward the desolate area south of the city. "Downtown."

But I could see we were clearly not headed into the city, and my imagination knew no limits. Did they plan to kidnap us and hold us for ransom? I wondered why we had foolishly placed our lives in the hands of someone we didn't know.

Finally, I mustered enough courage and inquired, "Downtown is in the other direction. Why are we driving away from downtown?"

She was shocked by this critical bit of information. Being a novice English speaker, she assumed that since south was downward on a map, "downtown" meant south of the city. She explained that they lived in a new high-rise development, and we were almost there.

Sure enough, we soon saw tall buildings jutting up in the distance and pulled into the parking lot. My stomach relaxed, and I took my hand off the door handle.

They ushered us up the elevator to their apartment, where we were treated like a visiting American president and his wife. Another couple had been laboring for hours on an eight-course feast. In their culture, the more honored the guest, the more dishes served. A dining room table arrived while we ate, which they had ordered especially for our visit.

Our drive home was much more relaxed because we knew them better and could trust them. We developed a good friendship, and eventually, she came to know Jesus.

When I began my spiritual journey over 50 years ago, my level of trust in Jesus was as uncertain as my assessment of our new friends' intentions during our ride "downtown." Sometimes, I feared the worst if I gave Him control.

This nail-biting ride with strangers led me to whimsical musing. Would I have jumped into that car if Jesus were behind the wheel? Absolutely! I know He will carefully and lovingly choose the places He takes me.

I had to first get to know Him and whether I could trust Him behind the wheel. Once I decided He was trustworthy behind the wheel of my life, the adventures He has taken me on have been beyond my imagination!

Reflect:

Who is behind the "steering wheel" of your life? What do you need to know about Jesus to be able to trust Him to drive, if He's not already?

Consider:

"The thief's purpose is to steal and kill and destroy. My purpose is to give them a rich and satisfying life."

—John 10:10 NLT

You can only trust someone as much as you know them. How could you get to know Jesus better?

CHAPTER 7

THE LOOSE ARM

Despite the crowds pressing in around my mom and me, I felt as carefree as any four-year-old could. We wove our way down the central aisle of a busy department store and all I could see were pant legs and shoes shuffling and shoving. I kept my eyes riveted on the bottom of my mother's familiar dress. As long as I kept close to that dress, all was well.

Just then, there was a clearing in the leg jungle, and a mannequin ahead distracted my attention. *I wonder what the skin feels like.* A short-sleeved blouse left inviting arms hanging perfectly within any curious child's reach.

I intended to just touch the hand as we passed, but the unthinkable happened.

The whole arm detached.

I stood there in horror, with an extra arm extending from my hand.

I broke it! What do I do now?

This early attempt to reach outside my comfort zone was obviously traumatic. I froze, staring at the wayward arm while my unsuspecting mother charged forward through the mayhem.

At some point, I realized my mom's familiar dress was nowhere to be found. I felt honor-bound not to separate this poor mannequin from her arm by taking it with me to search for my mom. So I stood there, arm in hand. No one rushing by even noticed the little girl holding a mannequin arm. Perhaps they thought I was a mannequin, too?

The arm became heavier and heavier. Then, the panic-stricken face of a sales clerk appeared in the distance, forcing her way toward me against the flow of traffic as she searched both sides of the aisle. Not far behind, pushing through like a football quarterback, was dear ol' Mom.

Judging by Mom's reaction, seeing me standing there with that silly mannequin arm was the best thing she had seen in a long time. The sales clerk reclaimed the arm, and as far as I know, the mannequin's appendage and her dignity were restored.

This story reminds me of a foundational principle I learned about adventure. Life went smoothly as long as I walked alongside my mother, but things fell apart when I stepped out of her protective circle.

It applies to us and our Heavenly parent, too. Adventure just for the thrill of adventure isn't as rewarding as when it's for God's higher good. If you are taking risks into the unknown, you are better off walking alongside the all-powerful, all-knowing Father and letting Him lead you instead of facing the unfriendly masses alone.

Reflect:

How could you determine if God is guiding you into a particular adventure?

Consider:

"Don't be afraid, for I am with you. Don't be discouraged, for I am your God. I will strengthen you and help you. I will hold you up with my victorious right hand."

— Isaiah 41:10 NLT

How would knowing God is walking alongside you make a difference as you step out of your comfort zone?

CHAPTER 8

WALKING THE PLANK

Do I really want to do this?

The wooden plank quivered as I tested my weight on the end, trying not to notice the scary water-filled pit below. I hesitatingly inched across the wobbly board until I reached my destination: a cereal box on the pantry shelf.

My father never lacked creative ideas. Some worked, and some didn't. When I was about nine years old, Dad was confident he could dig a basement under our house. This didn't help my parents' already-strained relationship.

He started in the pantry, which was about eight feet by five feet. A wall of shelves hung on the right, and the water heater sat in the back left corner. Before long, my father discovered it may have been better to build a swimming pool because water spurted up with every shovel of dirt he removed.

Dad abandoned the project after digging a four-foot-deep hole under the whole pantry, but he didn't quite get around to replacing the floor. Family members thought twice about getting a snack, including me.

Our bathroom floor also had an unstable foundation. Six children's unrestrained bath times and a few plumbing leaks had caused rot in sections of the plywood flooring. My father "temporarily" patched the decaying boards by throwing down a piece of plywood on top of the worst area between the tub and the toilet. It creaked and dipped a little with each step.

Most of the time, I didn't think about the disintegrating floor. Tip-toeing carefully when brushing one's teeth seemed normal. But I shuddered whenever I stopped to imagine the wood giving way and the toilet or sink taking a quick exit under the house, with me not far behind.

The floor's "temporary fix" stayed that way until we moved three years later. Amazingly, the toilet never took that final plunge. And the pantry's water heater levitated over the floorless floor without cracking off of the wall pipes to which it desperately clung.

There's a sense of uncertainty when the floor beneath you, which is supposed to be solid, isn't; and it's unsettling when your family can't offer the stability needed for a secure emotional foundation. So as I grew up, I avoided the unpredictable and the unknown.

I told you I'm an unlikely adventurer, didn't I?

I am not proud of my humble beginnings. Then why am I telling you about them? Because as you read the chapters ahead, I want you to know it is remarkable, even supernatural, that I am who I am today and have dared to live the life God led me on. Jesus freed me from my self-made cocoon and some of the limitations from my past when He and His unchanging truths became the firm foundation underneath me.

How incredible that our extraordinary God, the architect and builder of our lives, chooses us to be His children. Any ordinary person who follows the Great Adventurer will experience the incredible adventures He created them for.

Reflect:

What's uncertain in your life right now? How does this uncertainty keep you from moving forward?

Consider:

"Truly He is my rock and my salvation; He is my fortress, I will never be shaken."

— Psalm 62:2 NIV

If you knew you could trust your uncertainties to a God who is completely reliable, what would be the first thing you would do?

CHAPTER 9

STEPPING THROUGH THE DOORWAY

Does God expect me to wear clothes from the dumpster and read hymnbooks for excitement?

Well, okay, that's an exaggeration. But as a teenager, I did have strange ideas about what God expected from His followers and what it meant to be a Christian. My impression wasn't good. I thought people with a strong faith usually called on God because they didn't have the energy or ambition to take care of things for themselves. They were the kind who sat back and watched soap operas, expecting God to do the work for them.

Paradoxically, I always believed in God but kept Him tucked in my back pocket for emergencies only. I wanted to blend in with everyone else and not get too deep into this Jesus stuff my mom talked too much about. Besides, if He were as powerful as the Bible said, there was no telling what He would do to my life if I got too close to Him. When I grew old, I would probably get "religious," too.

It never occurred to me to investigate who Jesus was as a historical figure. I didn't know being a Christian had a solid foundation of historical facts to support Jesus' claims to be God and His resurrection from the dead. No one had told me that being a Christian is a friendship with the Lord of the universe, not a lifestyle of rules to hammer out myself.

I carefully crafted my own little universe which I controlled by working hard, following the rules, and having a guy to fall back on. I earned honors in academics, writing, and art, and high school graduation found me with a full scholarship to the state university of my choice. But there was one problem. The foundation of my heart and my life purpose were riddled with holes. I had no clue what I wanted to do with my life, let alone what university to attend.

I chose the university with the shortest drive from home and from my boyfriend's college. I longed for someone to fill my empty heart and provide a stable floor underneath me. I had no idea my misconceptions about God were keeping me from the very Person I was searching for.

When two friendly strangers approached me in the university cafeteria and told me how I could know Jesus, I had to decide how to respond. Was I willing to let go of my predictable, known world and move toward a mostly unknown God?

The two collegians didn't fit my negative stereotype; in fact, I admired them. Bonnie and Sue dressed stylishly and were doing exciting things like traveling to Florida for Spring Break. I saw peace and joy in their lives, which I wanted.

Sue told me simple Bible truths that broke through the lies I believed about God. He wanted to fill my love tank to overflowing, but choosing my own way separated me from Him and His love. So God came in the form of a perfect man, Jesus. He died on the cross to pay for everything I have ever done wrong, then rose from the dead. If I believed in Him, I could know Him and His love and have His Spirit live inside of me. He had a wonderful plan for me—an incredible adventure—if I chose to trust and obey Him.

It took six months for me to realize how messed up my self-made world was and to decide I wanted to know the Jesus my two new friends described. I went to church for the first time in years and prayed, "Jesus, if

I can know you and if you have a better plan for my life, I'm interested."

I took a risk when I asked the God of the universe to take the steering wheel of my life without knowing what He would do in response. My book, *Tire Tracks,* describes my hesitant first steps of faith and Jesus's incredible faithfulness in the years that followed.

Trusting Jesus turned out to be the best decision I ever made. He is the solid foundation I was searching for and brought a life overflowing with adventures of every kind, good and bad. I continue to learn what Jesus meant when He said in John 10:10, "I came that they might have life and have it abundantly."

Jesus knows all about adventure. The Great Adventurer left His perfect comfort zone in heaven when He came to earth, so He could lead us to places we never imagined we would go. He has used my steps of faith to transform me into a still hesitant but sometimes wild adventurer.

Reflect:

What three words come to mind if asked to describe a Christian? Where did you get the information that your impression is based on?

Consider:

"Jesus said to him, 'I am the way, and the truth, and the life; no one comes to the Father except through Me.'"

—John 14:6 NASB

If Jesus is the truth, like this verse says, why not take a minute to pray and ask Him to show you any misconceptions about who He is and what the Christian life is like?

Is There a Strong Man Holding Your Ladder?

The climber in this photo is literally putting his life in the other man's hands. The top man is in big trouble if the bottom man is not strong enough to hold the ladder up. Before he clambered onto the first rung, the climber needed to know and trust the man underneath well enough to be confident he could hold his weight while suspending the ladder in the air.

Adventure requires change and unknowns, which are often uncomfortable and even scary. Start with a foundation so strong and unchanging that the most critical elements in your life remain the same no matter what. This will give you the courage to dive wholeheartedly into your adventures.

Suggested Prayer:

Dear God, what or whom am I trusting? What foundation am I standing on? Is it solid? Many things seem to offer hope, strength, and confidence, but sometimes I feel disappointed. Show me who You are and whether I can trust You to be unchanging even if that which is familiar changes. In Jesus' name, amen.

68
武天平

SECTION TWO

Release

I marveled at how the rhythm of life at the large north market ebbed and flowed in the less-than-ideal helter-skelter of bargaining and buying. Merchants haggled, cars and three-wheeled bicycles jostled and competed for space at crowded loading blocks, and street vendors shouted today's lunch special.

Then I came across this young man. He was so carefree—or exhausted—he picked a spot, ignored the noise and traffic, and slept. Over the years, I have encountered just a few people who could doze at will. What was their secret?

How can some effortlessly drift off to sleep when for others, snoozing is elusive even with climate-controlled rooms, sleeping pills, window-darkening curtains, and the perfectly shaped pillow?

Perhaps the answer reminds us of the second ingredient required for your great adventure: Letting go.

CHAPTER 10

Dried Fish for Breakfast

"Large American Breakfast Buffet Served!"

My heart leaped and my mouth watered as I read the sign in our conference hotel lobby. Since we had arrived in East Asia three weeks earlier, I experienced more unfamiliar foods than I cared to remember. Then we left for a conference in Thailand, which meant another new menu of unusual dishes.

This buffet would be a welcome piece of home.

I tossed and turned all night, imagining the foods I would pile on my plate. I could almost taste soft waffles with syrup cascading over the sides and an omelet overloaded with ham, onions, and cheddar cheese. As soon as the sun rose, I rushed to breakfast. The scene that greeted me, though, can only be described as cruel false advertising.

It was indeed a large buffet. But it was not American.

I gasped at this smorgasbord of scary-looking foods: hot peppers, mushy rolls filled with shredded tuna or black beans, and unidentifiable concoctions I was certain would crawl off the platter if stared at long enough. And dried fish. Yes, dried fish. For breakfast. A few rubbery pancakes, granola, yogurt, and what looked like yesterday's scrambled eggs hid behind the pickled vegetables.

Swallowing my expectations along with my eggs and roll, I enjoyed the coffee and began to strategize on how to make this buffet taste more American. Laying half asleep that night, I remembered eating yogurt and cereal almost every day in America. Suddenly, I was wide awake. Yogurt topped with granola would almost be like breakfast on my screened porch back home. Morning couldn't come fast enough.

Arriving at the buffet, every dish was full except for one. The yogurt. It was completely empty, and the waiter informed me there was no more.

To my surprise and embarrassment, tears welled up in my eyes. *How could they be out of the one thing I was counting on, the one thing from my safe, familiar world that I wanted to cling to?* My persistent efforts to recreate "home" had crumbled in a heap.

I left everything and moved halfway around the world. Was a stinkin' little bowl of yogurt too much to ask for?

After I calmed down, it was as if a gentle voice said, "Nancy, you came here to be part of their world, just as I came to be part of your world. You must stop looking for how things were, or you won't see what I have in front of you today!"

So, I promised God I'd sample a new food each day. Some dishes didn't taste nearly as bad as they looked and were actually delicious with scrambled eggs.

I never gathered enough courage to try dried fish or hot peppers. And I still had yogurt and granola whenever possible. But instead of seeing these foods as a way to cling to the old and familiar, they became a treat to enjoy occasionally while I embraced my new normal.

I began to learn we must surrender what's safe and familiar to make room for His new adventures.

Reflect:

What are you hanging onto that makes risking new things hard? How can you make room for the new?

Consider:

"Therefore, since we are surrounded by such a huge crowd of witnesses to the life of faith, let us strip off every weight that slows us down, especially the sin that so easily trips us up. And let us run with endurance the race God has set before us."

— Hebrews 12:1 NLT

What might be some unique accomplishments ahead in "the race God has set before you?" Check out "Taking Off on Your Great Adventure" at the end of this book for ideas.

How does the image created by this verse help you see the importance of dealing with things that weigh you down?

CHAPTER 11

Lost in the Grocery Store

It was time.

Two weeks after arriving in East Asia, I gathered my shopping list and my courage and set off alone to explore the massive department store. Little did I know the adventure that awaited me between the disposable shoe covers and black bean bread.

I took a deep breath, entered the main door, and wove my way through the crowds milling around the small shops that lined the inside perimeter of the store. *How can it be this hard to find the department store entrance?* Finally, I spotted a moving sidewalk. This carried me to the upper floor and the point of entry.

I grabbed a cart and tried to look like I knew what I was doing. *Where is the household section? Do they even sell bed sheets?* I forged my way ahead.

I couldn't see past the mountains of merchandise, and my vision was even more obscured by a steady stream of customers excitedly examining an endless assortment of big-screen televisions and cellphones. Just when I thought I had searched down every aisle, I discovered a whole new section. *Still no sheets.* I swallowed my growing sense of panic that something very familiar—shopping—had become very foreign.

Finally, success! I found the sheets. An enthusiastic store clerk delivered what I am sure was a great sales pitch, but I didn't understand a word of it. My heart sank as I examined the sheets more closely. They were not labeled with the familiar king, queen, and single. They were marked by how many centimeters wide and long they were. The metric system was as clear to me as the local language, so we would need to sleep without sheets until I figured this out.

Ready to head to the first-floor supermarket, a guard stopped me from going back down the way I came up and pointed back into the store. *There must be another moving sidewalk that goes down, but where?*

I wondered and wandered. The exit signs all led to employee break rooms. If the workers were not all so respectful, I might have been tempted to believe these signs to nowhere were for the employees' amusement. They could watch daze-faced newcomers ramble endlessly through the maze with their hopes dashed each time an exit sign led to nowhere.

It is a profound kind of lonely to be in the midst of wall-to-wall people with no one you can talk to.

My next 40 minutes felt more like I was one of the Israelites wandering aimlessly in the desert with Moses for 40 years. *How do you hide an escalator? And how could I admit to anyone that I couldn't find my way out of a grocery store?*

I had begun to discover that living overseas sometimes tore into shreds any pride and self-confidence. This increased my prayer life considerably.

Things took on a more urgent tone because, by now, I needed a restroom. Badly. How to say, "Where is the toilet?" in their language was hidden in the remote recesses of my brain and refused to be retrieved. This was unfortunate timing for a memory lapse.

It finally occurred to me to ask an employee if he spoke English. The clerk was more than happy to help and called over another worker. He told me in broken English to proceed to the far-left corner.

There it was, in all its hidden glory. Finally, I came face to face with a very narrow moving sidewalk. It was buried behind the crowds examining sleek-shine shampoo and face-whitening masks. I triumphantly proceeded down the moving ramp, trying to look unruffled.

At the bottom, the tantalizing odors of endless bins of dried seaweed, hot peppers, exotic spices, dried fish, and fresh baked goods filled my nostrils. I quickly corralled the food we needed, thanks to bilingual signs, and successfully paid at the checkout counter. Now I just needed to make it home to my restroom.

My heart flooded with a song of victory, and I foolishly thought my adventure for today was almost over. I had no idea the worst was yet to come.

Reflect:

When you experience difficulties, do you see them as learning opportunities or things to be avoided? How could you view them more as an adventure?

Consider:

"And He said to them, 'Follow Me, and I will make you fishers of men.' "
— Matthew 4:19 NASB

When Jesus called the disciples, they were not yet qualified, but Jesus promised to train them. Is there something you sense God is calling you to but you don't feel qualified? What is one way you could become better equipped for this new venture?

CHAPTER 12

Taxis and Buses and Scooters, Oh My!

I had successfully completed my first trip alone to the grocery store. Now, how would I get home?

The only "taxi" waiting at the curb was a haggard elderly woman pulling a rusted cart with her old bicycle. The seat was a worn wooden board resting on top of the crumbling cart. It held my life at its mercy for the next death-defying eight minutes. I was not prepared for how this trip home would thrust me into near collisions with every type of transportation used in the history of Asia. And her flimsy wagon ranked at the bottom of the food chain.

That little lady sure could pedal a bicycle! I watched wide-eyed as we dodged a truck that swerved in front of us. Cars appeared out of nowhere. I felt the warm exhaust all around me and choked on the fumes. *Note to self: Avoid rides home at rush hour.*

Taxis, bicycles, buses, and motor-scooter versions of rickshaws zigged and zagged around us as we all raced to reach the same empty spot on the road ahead. I prayed nonstop and clung tightly to the iron sidebars of this makeshift seat, as if my grip would keep me from catapulting into chaos in the event of a collision. My need for a bathroom suddenly ranked as the least of my worries.

When I caught sight of the park below our apartment window, I rejoiced my ride from h*ll was almost over. I gave the woman twice her usual fare since I felt sorry she had to lay her life on the line to make a living. Then, I steadied wobbly legs and piled my bags into the wobbly cart at our front gate. Peter lugged our groceries up the six flights to our apartment.

I slept well that night.

There were valuable lessons I learned through my maiden voyage home from the department store. First, being stretched out of my comfort zone is a gift. Instead of becoming hardened like peanut brittle, change keeps me elastic. It reminds me I am not the center of the universe and that other ways to do things exist. Living outside of the familiar motivates me to learn new skills.

Second, I felt a growing sense of victory as I tackled practical ways to accept and adjust to our new home instead of trying to make it feel like America. I carried a list of translated phrases with me everywhere.

Third, despite the scary aspects of this adventure, it made me feel alive. I loved to see and learn new things and chuckled to myself that my adult children would be shocked by their mother's daring adventures.

A sense of wonder flooded me over the transformation the Lord brought about in me. I used to avoid anything that remotely resembled a safety risk. He supplied the power for me to rise above my fears to accomplish His plan for my life.

Fear and peace coexisted because I knew I was where God wanted me. The safest place lies in the center of God's will. Protected in the palm of His hand, with His almighty fingers gently curled around me, is always the best place to abide.

Reflect:

Would you get into the lady's cart in this story? Why or why not?

Consider:

"Don't be afraid, for I am with you. Don't be discouraged, for I am your God. I will strengthen you and help you. I will hold you up with my victorious right hand."

— Isaiah 41:10 NLT

How confident are you that you are safe in God's hands? What might He be calling you to do that would mean letting go of trying to control your safety?

CHAPTER 13

A Parade of Sticky Angels

My shoulders still ached from carrying yesterday's groceries up the six flights of stairs to our apartment, but I had a bigger task in front of me that day: carting a pile of household items up the stairs. My friend had taken me to a home goods store where I hit the jackpot with a broad assortment of items needed for our new home. I filled the checkout conveyor belt with saltshakers, trashcans, cooking pots, and pillows. What a stash!

As we paid and packed up my treasures, it suddenly hit me that such success was not without a price. There were the stairs. Six flights suddenly seemed like sixty. Thinking about those 120 stairs made me wish I had not had such a successful shopping trip.

We arrived at my apartment complex and I heaped the treasures into one of the tenant shopping carts. The guards looked confused by my request for help. *Was something lost in the translation? Or perhaps they chose not to understand since it involved moving out of their comfortable office chairs?*

Living overseas required much more leaning on our Heavenly Father than back home, even for simple things. Peter was in class, so I asked God to please provide help getting all this stuff up to our apartment. Pushing the cart through the courtyard, a supernatural peace flooded my soul. I just knew that somehow He would provide because He is a good Father.

The heavy cart from the front gate bump-bumped over the brick driveway towards the very last stretch before the stairs. While I like to plan everything beforehand, sometimes Jesus waits until the exact moment to provide.

As I rounded the bend, three home-schooled sisters were just standing around. The ten-year-old straddled her bike as if they were waiting for me to arrive. The seven-year-old held two peanut butter and jelly sandwiches in one hand and her handlebars in the other. Peanut butter and jelly slowly oozed from the edges like a lava flow. The five-year-old gave me a big grin that revealed two missing teeth framed by jelly-smeared lips.

I asked the oldest one if she could help carry a few items. All three girls immediately and enthusiastically jumped into action. Another five-year-old pulled up on her bike and grabbed an armful, too.

There I was with a parade of "angels," holding their sticky sandwiches in one hand and my bags in the other. They wouldn't let me carry a thing. With great relief and thankfulness to our creative Father and my parade of angels, I walked up the stairs completely empty-handed. I can still see the sheer delight and pride on their faces as we all marched with determination up six flights.

"Would your mom object if I got you some ice cream?" I asked, once we got to my doorway.

"She would object, so no thank you!" All three of them smiled as if to say they didn't want to accept a reward and ruin the satisfaction of helping out. With angelic smiles and giggles, they were halfway down the stairs and jumping on their bicycles, sandwiches still in hand.

As I delighted in my store finds, I thought about how faithful God is. He blessed both the receiver and the giver. The way He provided looked different than what I expected. He not only provided help for me up the stairs but also allowed young children to experience the joy of giving and of seeing they can make a difference, peanut butter and jelly sandwiches and all.

Reflect:
If you were confident that God would provide whatever you need when you need it, what would your next step forward be?

Consider:
"And my God will meet all your needs according to the riches of his glory in Christ Jesus."

— *Philippians 4:19 NIV*

What would you like God to provide today?

CHAPTER 14

THE JUGGLING JUDGES

How had we gotten into this?

Peering at the students flooding into the tiered auditorium that stretched endlessly upward sent a shiver up my spine. Peter and I reluctantly sat down in the honored front-row judges' section next to the chairman of this Asian university's English department.

It had started simply enough. We agreed to ask each of the twenty speech contestants a follow-up question. *How hard could that be?* However, when we walked through the auditorium doorway, we were instantly promoted to "distinguished judges" because two of their judges were not able to attend. Now we had to juggle thinking of a question to ask immediately after each speech while simultaneously evaluating their performances in several categories.

As we received our crash course on the judging process and organized our score sheets, the emcee interrupted, "Can you conclude the event today with a summary of your thoughts about the performances?" I swallowed hard. Here was our third ball to juggle. Would there be more?

Many of the students had never met a native English speaker. As Americans living in East Asia, we were given great respect just for breathing. Since they considered us "celebrities," the moderator thought it made sense for us to give out the awards. Oh, and present a closing speech. One ball to juggle had grown to five: distinguished judge, clever questioner, award giver, event evaluator, and speaker.

After I sent up an urgent prayer for God's help, the fast-paced contest began. We assumed we would have time during the award ceremony at the end to scribble down something for our closing thoughts. But God knew there would be another unexpected twist in the road, and He prepared the way.

A three-hour whirlwind of excellent speeches followed, offering us a window into their world. God somehow enabled us to ask our questions and hand in each speech evaluation within the ten seconds it took for the next contestant to begin.

My mind shifted into fast-forward while we juggled. I have no idea how, other than the supernatural work of God, but a clear outline for our closing speech popped into my mind. I jotted it down, and it was a good thing I did.

As we sat with pens poised to judge the twentieth candidate, they suddenly announced, "The twentieth contestant was not able to attend, so one of our American judges is going to give a speech instead."

Right. Now.

I rose calmly with my scribbled scrap paper and the amazing confidence of someone who had prepared for weeks. There was a great sense of God's Presence in the room as I spoke, congratulating them for their excellent performances and expressing our love for the people in their country. God was sufficient indeed, and I sensed an even greater warmth and respect from the audience after I spoke.

We don't always know ahead of time what may be required of us. But we do know that God, who dwells outside of time, will equip us for whatever we need.

He juggles the planets and stars in their orbit. How difficult can it be for Him to help juggle the twists and turns in the lives of two desperate judges?

Reflect:

Think of a time when you were suddenly expected to do more than you were planning on. How did you handle it?

Consider:

"Very truly I tell you, whoever believes in me will do the works I have been doing, and they will do even greater things than these, because I am going to the Father."

—John 14:12 NIV

After Jesus's death and resurrection, the unlimited power of the God of the universe came to live inside of every believer. How does knowing this impact your confidence in what you (with the Holy Spirit inside of you) are capable of?

CHAPTER 15

The Power of Powerlessness

"Keep to the left!" I shouted as the driver once again drifted toward the oncoming highway traffic.

"Back toward the right!" we corrected him as he headed left toward the row of enormous trees that lined the highway. This terrifying ride to the airport was not the way we wanted to remember our vacation time in Thailand.

As the time for our flight's departure ticked closer, I thought about how our middle school daughter would be waiting for us at our home airport when she returned from her school trip.

"We're almost there! Just 500 meters!" he repeatedly told us, as we watched planes above head in the opposite direction. He was taking us away from the airport, and his driving deteriorated more.

Then we realized our driver was struggling to not fall asleep. I found myself thinking that when they gave our children the car wreckage remains, at least the photos on our phones would show them our last days together were happy ones.

When we finally approached a village, Peter wisely ordered the driver to let us out immediately at the closest police station. The police were unmoved by our plight and all but yawned in our faces. While Peter tried to find another ride, I stood with our luggage. Trying to be strong, I tried not to watch the clock. I thanked the Lord that He was still in control and tried to convince myself that I was not worried. But in the back of my mind, I wondered how He would get us to the airport on time.

The clock ticked on until reality hit me. *We really might miss this flight, and our daughter would be alone at the airport.* My stoic pretense cracked.

I began to cry.

An incredible thing happened. My tears produced the same all-hands-on-deck action you would expect from a tsunami alert. The police officers bolted over with great alarm.

"What's wrong?? Where are you going?" they asked in broken English. Thailand prides itself on being the "Land of Smiles," so apparently it sets off a distress alert when you aren't smiling!

Three officers sprang into action. At breakneck speed, they threw our luggage into the back of their pickup truck. Lights flashing, they rushed us to the airport in record time.

Our heroes enthusiastically asked for photos with us before we raced off to the check-in counter. They were especially pleased that a smile replaced my tears.

I was smiling because we had escaped alive from that crazy driver.

I was smiling because God had done what I had concluded was impossible.

I was smiling because God brought results through my vulnerable and needy tears, not through my trying to convince myself and others that I was strong when I was not. He certainly honors those who resemble the saints in the Hebrews 11 "Faith Hall of Fame." However, He is the most moved when we come to Him exactly as we are, whether we are full of faith or full of fear.

And that's a lot to smile about!

Reflect:
When you have a problem, do you pretend to be strong or ask for help?

Consider:
"But he said to me, 'My grace is sufficient for you, for my power is made perfect in weakness.' Therefore, I will boast all the more gladly about my weaknesses, so that Christ's power may rest on me."

— 2 Corinthians 12:9 NIV

Why do you think we need to be weak in order for Jesus' strength to give us the power to try something new? What would it look like for you to let go of trying to be strong when you aren't?

CHAPTER 16

The Mysterious Tea Leaf Bungler

Where did this mysterious bag come from?

I returned from running errands to discover a large brown bag of tea leaves in the center of my white kitchen counter. I thought my friend had left them there, but she assumed they belonged to another visitor. The second visitor thought they were mine. Eventually, we figured out it did not belong to any of us.

When you live in a country with "many eyes," you must assume there may be uninvited guests from time to time when you are away from your apartment. But it is a strange feeling when tangible evidence appears on your kitchen counter next to the toaster oven. *Was there a logical explanation, or had we been visited by a bungling spy who forgot his bag of tea leaves?*

Another time, after we returned from vacation, the locks on two of our file cabinet drawers were broken. Nothing was missing, including money. It could be that we just didn't notice before we left that two drawers didn't work anymore. Or it could be….

And what about that small wire circle with a translucent membrane that appeared on our dining room floor one day, as if it had fallen from somewhere? Was it from a recording device or something random that we brought in on a shoe?

Public cameras were commonplace in buildings, driveways, elevators, and hallways. Every day, we lived in a world of questions. There were always things that either proved someone was watching, following, or listening. Or they were just coincidences.

My husband Peter changed the apartment door lock. But if the tea leaf bungler wanted to return for his tea leaves, he would figure out a way. Our new lock just offered an illusion of security. Our real protection came from the powerful God of angel armies. As the framed message on our bedroom wall declared, "The will of God will never lead you where the grace of God cannot keep you."

He kept us overseas for as long as He wanted us there—in spite of the elusive tea leaf burglar.

Reflect:
How would you react if you found mysterious tea leaves on your counter?

Consider:
"The time is coming when everything that is covered up will be revealed, and all that is secret will be made known to all. Whatever you have said in the dark will be heard in the light, and what you have whispered behind closed doors will be shouted from the housetops for all to hear!"

— Luke 12:2,3 NLT

Does it make you feel comforted or concerned that there are no secrets with God? Why?

CHAPTER 17

Playing Visa Monopoly

(Important Disclaimer: Every government has its version of bureaucratic red tape, so you can fill in the blank with the country of your choosing.)

I love taking care of visas at the last minute—about as much as I love a root canal without painkillers.

But, the Lord had in mind another lesson of faith, patience, and dependence on Him as we applied to renew our visas to stay in our host country for another year.

We had to wait until our daughter returned from her class trip. This would be a tight squeeze, but the visa office said that if we applied the very next day, our visas would be back the day before we left for America for the summer.

So early Monday, Peter headed to the visa office downtown, having gathered our passports, two new photos of each of us, our daughter's notarized birth certificate signed by America's Attorney General Condoleezza Rice, a translated birth certificate, our notarized marriage license signed by Hillary Clinton, a translated copy of our marriage license, a letter from the local police, our lease, completed application forms, Peter's medical form saying he is healthy, copies of our airline ticket itinerary, and an official letter from Peter's school with a red stamp. All papers taken seriously **must** have a red stamp.

"This application has been done in blue," the lady at the desk observed.

"Yes… the instructions on the application say black or blue ink," Peter replied.

"That's not ink. It's ballpoint pen," she replied.

Then what do you call that thick blue stuff inside of my pen that leaves an indelible stain? Peter wisely did not verbalize what he was thinking.

Do not pass go, do not collect visa. Fill out the application again with *black ink.*

Back to the clerk. This time she observed that Peter's passport had no more empty visa pages.

Do not pass go, do not collect visa. Go directly to embassy for additional passport pages.

So Peter headed across the city to the embassy. By now, the visa office was closed.

Day one is over. No visa.

Early the next morning, Peter skipped breakfast and flew out the door to the visa office again.

"Where is your wife's medical clearance form?" the now-familiar lady at the desk asked. "She must go to our official medical clinic for the red-stamped medical approval form. But it is only open mornings."

It didn't matter that I had a full day of exams at a very thorough wellness clinic in Thailand just three months earlier. It didn't matter that I had a letter on hospital letterhead declaring my health status and signed by the doctor. It didn't matter that Peter gave them the same kind of form as mine, from the exact same day and exact same Thailand hospital, with *no* red stamp.

But his was acceptable. Mine was not.

Do not pass go, do not collect visa. Go directly to clinic - Tomorrow morning. Pay $75.

Day two is over. No visa.

I waited in line the next morning at the medical clinic. I showed them the eight pages of detailed medical test results from Thailand, which they looked at with disdain. I gave them my money and my blood and took several tests.

"Come back tomorrow afternoon for the official stamped paper," The lady at the desk declared.

"This is an emergency! I must get my visa before we leave!" I objected.

"Come back this afternoon at 4:00," she says, adding two red stamps instead of one to the request form. This would be just enough time to rush back to the visa office before 5:00.

So we arrived promptly at 4:00. The apologetic woman behind the counter told us that the printer had broken, so the paper would not be ready until tomorrow.

Inside my secret chamber of hidden thoughts and feelings, I became the "ugly American." It was a good thing my local vocabulary was limited so that I wasn't tempted to share my frustration.

Do not pass go. Do not collect visa. Go directly home and pray. Hard.

Day three is over.

Meanwhile, somewhere along the line, Peter discovered that because our daughter was turning 18 in September, she had to apply separately as an adult. So he began gathering her application requirements while juggling the details for ours.

Her school needed a few days to process the necessary paperwork.

Come back in two days.

Then, the school's red stamp (required on any paper you want them to consider as being official) was out of red ink and had to be sent away to be refilled.

Do not pass Go. Do not collect visa. Miss a turn while waiting for stamp to be refilled.

After receiving the official paperwork, our daughter took time off school and met Peter downtown at the visa office.

"Doesn't she need a medical form?" I asked Peter beforehand, being painfully aware of that topic.

"No, it is not on the printed list of needed items they gave me at the visa office, and the school didn't say so either."

Can you guess what the office told Peter when they took in her visa application?

Do not pass Go. Do not collect visa. Go directly to clinic. Tomorrow. Tell your wife she was right.

Day four is over.

Our daughter had two days of school left, filled with exams, important review classes, and goodbyes to friends who were leaving. There was no morning she could spend at the medical clinic. Weighing all things, we made a decision.

Do not pay $75 for the clinic physical. Do not miss a turn at school. Get out of jail free.

Our daughter could pass "Go" by going directly to the clinic in the USA, where our insurance covered it. Instead of a school visa, we purchased a short-term tourist visa. This qualified her to go home to America for the summer. She could collect her school visa when we returned for the fall semester.

Peter submitted the final paperwork for himself and me, which was finally accepted! The lady at the desk promised to place the visas on a fast track to be ready on June 11th – the day before we left.

Game over.

We won! We won! We won!!

Reflect:
How do you react when you lose control of your plans?

Consider:
"The Lord will accomplish what concerns me; Your faithfulness, Lord, is everlasting; Do not abandon the works of Your hands."

— *Psalm 138:8 NASB*

How could this verse encourage you when things don't move forward in the ways you wish they did?

CHAPTER 18

THE EMPTY WALL

That day, I stared at an empty wall.

For as long as I could remember, the wall displayed the expanding story of our family history. In the center was our wedding picture with a gold cross above it, representing the One who brought us together and held us together. On both sides, photos celebrated our four children's babyhood up to proud graduation moments—moments too precious to be forgotten.

I reveled in this display for sixteen years every time I sat at our dining room table. All those faces smiled back at me as the framed memories grew. Pictures of birthday candles being blown out and Thanksgiving turkeys carved displayed our growing family history. Seeing the ongoing trail of family togetherness created a warm, secure feeling.

As we prepared our home for the renters who would live there while we were in East Asia, it occurred to me they wouldn't want a wall full of my family's photos. So, my treasures were carefully packed away, nail holes plastered, and the wall painted. Not a trace of evidence was left—just nothingness.

With the final sweep of the paintbrush, I was struck by an unexpected sense of extreme loss. Years of close moments with those I loved had been erased, and there was no certainty about what the future might bring. It brought home the reality that the door to an incredibly special chapter of my life was about to close. Our family and celebrations would never be the same since we would be living on different continents.

Our "say-something-nice-about-the-birthday-person-before-you-get-a-piece-of-cake" tradition would no longer be possible. No more Daniel stopping in for a cold drink and a brief visit after mowing our neighbor's lawn. No more Andrew taking his little sister to breakfast on Tuesdays, then chauffeuring her to school, or stopping by "just because." No more Julia's unannounced popping in when she was in the area.

While I knew God never asks us to give up something without replacing it with something He knows is better, I experienced a great sense of loss. I knew the Lord's grace would be there, but as I stared at that empty wall, it was hard to deal with this inevitable change.

Sometimes, God requires that we leave our homes and families for His name's sake (Matthew 19:29). We weren't the first ones to have done this. Anything of great value costs something, and leaving our family was the required price in order to offer God's incredible gift to those who have never heard.

Did I have second thoughts about following the Lord's lead? Absolutely not. But that doesn't mean there was no agony in the process.

If God gave His only Son so that I could know and enjoy eternal life, was it too much for Him to ask me to leave the future of my "Family Gallery" in His hands to orchestrate the chapters ahead as He saw fit? It gave me a glimpse into what our Heavenly Father suffered when He sent His Son far from His heavenly home so we could have a place with Him forever.

As I poured out my heart to Jesus, I was comforted by His reminder that just as the cross hung above all our family photos, the One who holds the power of the cross would continue to work in each family member. Jesus is the same yesterday, today, and forever. He would not stop being God in their lives just because we were halfway around the world. It gave them further opportunity to decide if Jesus' cross would be above their "life galleries" and the chance to turn to Him as their heavenly parent when we couldn't be here.

Weeks later, we zippered shut the last suitcase and headed on our way. Tenants moved in and made their own memories in what was once my sacred space.

No one could ever replace our own flesh and blood and special times with them. Being away never became easier. But God faithfully gave us new walls in our sixth-floor apartment overseas, which He filled with much laughter and deep connection.

New faces shining with eternal hope joined "God's forever family gallery" as we witnessed their spiritual births and growth in the warmth and security of those walls.

After ten meaningful years overseas, we moved back into our home again. The dining room wall has a fresh batch of photos that includes weddings, seven grandchildren, and our 45th anniversary.

Was there loss? Yes, definitely. But the gain by far outweighed what was lost.

This was God's intention all along.

Reflect:
What is the hardest thing for you as you consider following Jesus?

Consider:
"And everyone who has given up houses or brothers or sisters or father or mother or children or property, for my sake, will receive a hundred times as much in return and will inherit eternal life."

— Matthew 19:29 NLT

Is there anything you sense God is asking you to let go of so He can use you in significant ways?

CHAPTER 19

Closets We Run To

The darkness wrapped its familiar arms around me while I crouched with my arms wrapped around my knees. As a seven-year-old, this small closet was my friend. My older sister scrunched closely beside me in silent solidarity, staring at the closet curtain.

The floor was hard and cold in contrast to the warmth of sitting shoulder to shoulder. I wanted to melt into the hand-me-down clothes hanging above us. Our dolls huddled around us, innocently unaware of the turmoil one floor below.

In more lighthearted moments, we ran giggling to the protection of this closet when our father ate Limburger cheese. It was the only place in the whole house where the pungent odor didn't seem to penetrate. We wondered how a cheese could possibly taste good enough to endure that awful smell.

But on this occasion, the closet was a place to escape the shouting that exploded from the kitchen. The commotion charged around the corner, through the living room, up the stairs, and around the bend to our bedroom. This was the only place we knew to hide, but the angry bellowing forced its way into the closet's stillness.

I pictured my older brother, tight-lipped and stone-faced as he slumped in the chair, enduring this one-way "conversation." My father's face contorted with rage as he lectured my brother about his most recent unforgivable violation, not taking out the garbage.

Dad was a very colorful character and created a lot of fun when he was in a good mood. But watch out if he wasn't, especially when alcohol was involved. No wonder I saw the world as a scary, unpredictable place.

As the years passed, my parents divorced and children left the nest. My father mellowed and learned to control his anger; my older brother became a Christian. After experiencing the love and forgiveness of our Heavenly Father, he was able to forgive our father. Dad asked my brother if they could both forget the problems they had when he was a teenager, and they became close friends. Father and son ended up working together in Dad's security business.

Nothing can fully erase the impact of our childhood years. But I am in awe of how God used these difficult times to help lead all five of my siblings and me to Jesus. I treasure my close relationship with them now and the laughter and spiritual bonds we share. My older brother is the one who most often shares profound spiritual truths and videos.

No trauma can overrule God's power to save. Darkness does not have the final victory, but we do need to lay aside the lies we heard whispered while we lived in that darkness.

The lies I heard in the shadows included believing I was powerless. That my feelings and opinions didn't matter. I was not worth being protected or provided for. The only way I could be safe was to avoid risks and never do anything that attracted attention to myself. Most of the time I lacked the confidence to attempt new challenges, so I stayed in my small, safe cocoon where I could maintain control.

Not a likely candidate for authoring a book on adventure.

Then Jesus offered me His hand, as He did for Lazarus in the tomb many years ago. You can read about it in John 11:1-44. I learned I could let go of the old messages from my childhood. He led me out of my hiding place and into the front lines of the unseen conflict around us. There are times when old lies pop up and I need to lay them aside again. And again. Knowing I have the God of the universe on my side gives me the courage to follow Him where I wouldn't dare to go alone.

I am still cautious by nature and sometimes fall back into seeing the world as a scary place. That's when I run to Him and He reminds me of what is true. There's a vast difference between walking into unknown adventures alone and walking into what my wise and loving Heavenly Father knows He and I can handle together.

Jesus's ability to transform lives is magnified by the contrast between that little girl and the woman He has made me today. Living in His light is more unpredictable and out of my control, but oh, so much more interesting and meaningful! I am in awe of the life-changing power of the One who lives inside of me. He is in the business of replacing our dark lies with the liberating light of His Truth, freeing us to pursue His endless adventures.

Reflect:

Where do you hide? What lies keep you from becoming all God created you to be?

Consider:

"Forget the former things; do not dwell on the past. See, I am doing a new thing! Now it springs up; do you not perceive it? I am making a way in the wilderness and streams in the waste- land."

— Isaiah 43:18,19 NIV

What does this verse say to you about dealing with self-defeating lies from your past so you are free to advance in God's plan for your future? Sometimes, consulting a professional counselor is necessary.

What Bundle Do You Need to Drop?

This young man carried his big bundles during work hours and put them down before he slept. He blocked out the chaos around him and quickly dozed off.

Our noise and traffic are often on the inside. We drag the overstuffed backpacks of our complicated lives everywhere we go and then wonder why it's hard to make progress. Or to sleep.

Releasing things that hold us back is essential if we want to move forward. What loads do we need to let go of? Being in control. Wanting to know all the details. Fear of failure, rejection, what others think, to name a few. Unrealistic expectations. Unforgiveness. The way we've always done things. Demeaning past messages. Whatever we think will keep us safe.

Otherwise, our safe world where we sit on the throne can become a prison that keeps us from experiences and people God created for us to enjoy.

Suggested Prayer:

Thank You, Lord, for the new and exciting adventures You have planned for me! Remind me that adventure often brings the unexpected and is usually outside of my comfort zone. Show me anything I am clinging to that's in the way. I release it into Your hands to make room for the new. I confess that fear keeps me from taking reasonable risks. Thank You that Your plan will never lead me where Your grace cannot keep me. In the name of Jesus, amen.

SECTION THREE

Embrace

Utter devastation surrounded us as our busload of volunteers wove through the aftermath of an 8.0 earthquake. Yet, the villagers embraced what life had dealt them, good or bad, and jumped into action.

We would like to believe that adventure only involves pleasantly exciting experiences. The reality is there can be adventure in both the good and the bad.

Sometimes we are not looking for adventure; adventure finds us. When we have God as our solid foundation, we can embrace whatever comes our way and allow our faith to impact our attitude toward even uninvited adventures.

Peter and I were flabbergasted when we returned one or two months after this picture. With only the power of bare hands working together, these villagers removed piles of rubble and built the frameworks of new homes. They set a great example for us to embrace whatever life deals us.

CHAPTER 20

Expect the Unexpected

Kicking and screaming on the inside, I dressed for the wedding.

"Why in the world did Lu invite us to his friend's wedding, someone we don't even know? He probably thinks we want the cultural experience, but we have already been to several weddings," I complained to my husband Peter.

Wall-to-wall visits with people crammed the days leading up to the event. *I love meeting with my local friends. But after too much of a good thing, didn't I deserve time to come up for air? Wasn't Sunday supposed to be my day of rest?*

Peter conscientiously dressed for the special event, but the last thing I wanted to do was meet more new faces at some stranger's wedding.

Peter's and Lu's friendship had an unusual beginning only God could orchestrate. Several months earlier, Lu stood out in the crowded Thailand airport because he was limping badly. Peter helped him with his luggage before we boarded our flights for an overnight layover in Malaysia. As we buckled up for takeoff, we discovered Lu, his wife, and his daughter had seats across from us. He and Peter talked during the flight, and after we landed in Malaysia, we parted ways—until the next morning. When we prepared to board our flight back to where we lived, they were waiting in the same line. Lu's family lived in the same city!

Lu was on medical leave from an influential government position because of a knee injury. Peter visited him after surgery, and we hosted Lu and his wife at our home a few times. Now, Lu had invited us to some stranger's wedding. Peter had invested too much in this friendship for me to offend Lu by ignoring his invitation.

But I was not happy.

When we arrived at the wedding venue, Lu ran over to Peter and me. He wore an ornate red traditional costume and a grin that stretched from ear to ear. The big photo banner outside the restaurant revealed that Lu and his "wife" were the couple getting married! This important detail had been lost in our translation of his invitation.

Lu proudly escorted us through the huge banquet hall, past the crowds, to two seats reserved at one of the front tables. Now that his two honored foreign friends had arrived, the ceremony could begin.

Great fanfare, confetti, and cheering ensued, and then they reached the part of the ceremony where the couple bowed and honored their parents. We watched nonchalantly while the parents took turns speaking, until the emcee approached us. He informed us that Lu and his wife would like us, as his honored foreign guests…

To give a speech to the 200 people in the room.

In their language, if possible.

Oh, and our turn was next, the most honored position after their parents.

Two minutes from now.

We gulped, whispered a quick prayer ("Help!"), and then stood. Peter did an impressive job of greeting the audience in their language and congratulating his special friend. I added a few sentences, too.

I would have greatly insulted them if I had not come, especially when they counted on their "honored foreign friends" to be part of the ceremony. Perhaps that detail had been lost in the translation of the invitation, too.

During the reception, we enjoyed several meaningful conversations with new friends whom it was clear the Lord brought us there to meet. Their need to see Jesus through us was more urgent than my need for rest. Seeing Jesus's power inside of me do what I could not do in my own strength expanded my view of His greatness. My desire for a relaxing afternoon melted as He gave me compassion for these new friends.

Later that evening, I chuckled as I mentally replayed the events of the afternoon. What an adventure I would have missed if I had stayed home. Life following Jesus may sometimes be challenging, but it is not usually boring especially when sprinkled with God's surprises, and His humor.

At times you and I must say no in order to take care of our own needs. But sometimes when we lay aside our preferences in order to honor the greater good, by saying "yes" even when we want to say "no," Jesus fills our needs in better ways than we ever imagined.

Reflect:

When you have the opportunity to do something new, is your first response usually to say yes, or no? Why is this usually your reaction?

Consider:

"Be wise in the way you act toward outsiders; make the most of every opportunity."

— *Colossians 4:5 NIV*

What opportunity are you considering today? How can you make the most of it?

CHAPTER 21

LOVE AFFAIR AT THE ORPHANAGE

"Will you hold me, will you love me?" The baby's sobbing spoke loudly without words. Desperate eyes pleaded as they followed mine.

I instantly fell in love.

We were volunteering at the orphanage for disabled people, a task that was both emotionally draining and rewarding.

Guard your heart, my rational mind warned me on the drive there. *It will only bring heartache if you allow yourself to care too much.*

The staff worked around the clock to care for these children, but the orphanage was understaffed. These overwhelmed workers barely had time to tend to basic physical needs, so they were grateful when volunteers gave these little ones love and attention.

On that day, I followed the plaster-cracked stairwell down to the babies' floor. In the first room, four or five babies lay in cribs tightly packed next to each other.

Passing the doorway to the next room, a baby crying by the window caught my attention. "Baby X" had encephalitis, a condition where water around the brain causes the head to be unusually large. Framed by perfectly shaped facial features, his alert eyes peered upward and concentrated intensely on my face. I gazed down at this beautiful human being made in the image of God, probably abandoned by his parents because the orphanage was his only hope for medical treatment.

Baby X had recently been discharged from the hospital, so he and a baby with severe jaundice were in this room, separate from the others. It was heartbreaking that these two babies, who needed loving arms the most, were too fragile for outsiders to be allowed to hold.

I gently laid my hand on Baby X's chest and talked softly, praying for him. His crying immediately stopped. He stared at me wide-eyed like he had discovered an amazing new treasure, examining my face and delighting in every detail. In his short five months of life, he probably had very few opportunities to stare into the face of another human being. It tugged hard at my heart.

The clincher was when he intentionally placed his extra-long, delicate fingers—those of a concert pianist, for sure—on my hand. Then he rubbed back and forth on my skin, over and over again. He seemed delighted by the rare pleasure of touching human skin. This child had much love to give but no one to give it to.

I reluctantly left that afternoon but was haunted a thousand times by Baby X's face. While waiting to visit again the following month, I prayed for this dear little boy. I asked the Lord to give Baby X a chance to know His love and to be loved by parents who see him for who he is and not for his malformation. And perhaps, one day, he would learn to play the piano.

I mentally calculated what would need to happen for us to foster or adopt him, and discussed it with Peter. Sadly, orphanages usually didn't have legal custody of disabled children, so they would not be authorized to release him. And realistically, I would have no idea how to care for his medical needs.

The time finally came to return to the orphanage. I rushed downstairs to see my wide-eyed heartthrob and was greeted by…an empty crib.

He was gone.

There was no evidence he ever existed. No one could tell me what happened to him, but in my heart, I knew. Was mine the last caring face he saw before Jesus gathered him into His arms? The sheets were neatly folded, waiting for the next love-starved, imperfect little body.

It still stirs my emotions when I remember this little boy. Yes, I could have avoided pain if I had stoically distanced myself from his suffering, but I would have missed out on so much. I discovered it is better to embrace another human being in their neediness than to allow myself to become hardened to others' pain.

This adventure that took place within me involved taking the risk of embracing someone whose future I could not control. I grew in my realization of the tremendous power one person can have on another just by caring and giving appropriate touch. The priceless gift of God's compassion shown through me poured healing salve into the emptiness of Baby X's soul. I could not fill all his needs, but I made a difference with the few scoops of love I was able to offer.

Helping others who have desperate needs can tempt us with the heady feeling that we have power like God, rescuing someone in their distress; yet when we look around and realize it is impossible to put much of a dent in all the suffering, it is overwhelming to realize we are so unlike God, glaringly unable to make more than a dent.

So we can do what we can and trust God to fill in the rest.

Reflect:

When did you last risk embracing someone else's heart?

Consider:

"Then Jesus said, 'Come to me, all of you who are weary and carry heavy burdens, and I will give you rest.'"

— Matthew 11:28, NLT

What burdens are weighing you down today that Jesus is willing to carry for you? How could you be like Jesus and take the risk of helping to carry someone else's burdens?

CHAPTER 22

Trapped in the Bathroom Stall

"Help me! Help me!"

I frantically tried to slide the bathroom bolt open. It slid closed easily enough, but now it was not budging one iota. My nonchalant visit to the restroom at our friend's wedding felt like it had turned into a prison sentence. *Would anyone hear my cries? How long would it take for someone to notice I was missing?*

I determined that my only hope was to break the lock forcefully, so I slammed the door back and forth, back and forth. This loosened the screws which were wiggling slightly. I assumed this was from previous unfortunate victims. *Perhaps they never escaped and were buried under the floorboards.*

Hope welled up when two women entered and tried to tell me what to do. But my language skills were limited, and I was still banging that door back and forth to get the stupid bolt to budge.

I glanced up and was surprised to see a young lady bent upside down over the top of my stall. Reaching down, she pointed to a tiny round bump to the left of the bolt. Pushing it downward, the bolt effortlessly sprang open. So did the door.

It is precisely for this kind of moment—which can happen more often than we care to admit— that it is helpful to be able to laugh at yourself.

It also can be a distinct advantage not to understand the language well enough to translate their comments, which may have included, "Dumb foreigner!"

Reflect:

Why do you think some people can laugh at themselves while others get angry or embarrassed at their mistakes?

Consider:

"A cheerful heart is good medicine, but a broken spirit saps a person's strength."

— *Proverbs 17:22 NLT*

What is one thing about yourself that you would like to take less seriously, even laugh about?

CHAPTER 23

Bikes, Bites, and Buddhas

My anticipation soared as we mounted the hotel's complimentary bicycles and I imagined myself gliding through the peaceful Thailand countryside. Riding bikes back in our city was anything but relaxing, so I couldn't wait for an opportunity to push those pedals while on vacation.

Peter and I admired the flowering shrubs and sparkling lake as we pedaled down the empty road. But the mood changed quickly when we rounded the bend. Two vicious dogs charged toward us. Peter and I pedaled faster. I envisioned their drooling fangs wrapped around my ankle. By now, I discovered my bike had only one gear—slow—and one brake. Thankfully, these dogs stopped when we glided down the hill and left the boundaries of their property.

Our relief only lasted until the next corner.

I wasn't sure what was more concerning, the next big hill looming before us or a new pair of angry-looking black dogs waiting at the top. This second set of black canines vigilantly paced back and forth, planning their attack. We kept a close eye on them while we walked our bikes up the hill, and Peter wisely picked up a long stick. While we continued on the dusty road, he waved the stick menacingly. This kept the two hostile carnivores at bay.

In the distance, over the bridge to the left, a mysterious sea of orange drifted across the landscape. *What in the world could that be?*

As we pedaled closer, we realized the orange wave was a cluster of Buddhist monks in their traditional robes. This road was taking us right through their backyard! To our right was a flurry of orange laundry flapping in the wind, and to our left was their house. Twenty or so monks headed for their small porch and knelt to pray and meditate. I'm not sure who was more surprised, them or us.

Some openly watched in disbelief as two stick-waving foreigners plowed through their devotions and their laundry. Others gave sideways glares, keeping their heads straight ahead to hide their break in concentration. A few stragglers looked at us with indignation or quizzical expressions.

Leaving them to continue their rituals, we discovered the road had gone in a big circle. This meant we had to pass the home of the first two sharp-fanged beasts again. We stopped and prayed for Jesus' protection. With Peter still brandishing his stick, I felt secure as we approached.

To my relief, the two attackers were nowhere to be seen. No barking, no sharp choppers, no loss of limb. We breathed easier as we whizzed past and arrived safely back at the hotel. Our unusual countryside ride was over, but I had two new insights to mull over.

First, maybe bike riding while dodging scooters, buses, taxis, cars, and other wheeled creations back in our busy city was not so bad after all.

And second, if you are ever stuck in a tough place with fangs snapping at your heels, call on Jesus. He is the real "jaw-stopper!"

Reflect:

Do you think the unexpected adventure in this story was worth the risk involved? Why or why not?

Consider:

"You, dear children, are from God and have overcome them, because the one who is in you is greater than the one who is in the world."

— 1 John 4:4 NIV

What adventure into the unknown are you considering? How would it give you courage if you were convinced Jesus is greater than anyone and anything?

CHAPTER 24

Where are the Napkins?

Sometimes the small differences in living overseas caught me off guard more than the big ones. Let's face it, every day is made up of thousands of small moments, and our minds expect certain familiar objects to be a part of them. We learn about other lifestyles as well as our own, when some of those familiar elements are missing.

For example, silverware. *In which store aisle are they hiding the spoons, forks and knives?* It was unsettling. Then it hit me that I was in a culture that uses chopsticks. I eventually found a store with silverware, but we learned how to use chopsticks so we could relate to our new friends.

Dishcloths made of bamboo still fascinate me. How do they get the fibers so soft?

Then there were dinner napkins.

One day, I contemplated the elusiveness of napkins as my eyes searched up and down the long department store aisle in vain.

How could there be so many different rectangular packages of paper, but not one single square package of dinner napkins? Some of the rectangles were facial tissues, others were paper towels, and some were toilet paper. They were all made from melty-type paper that dissolves and shreds into nothingness when it gets wet. This makes terrible napkins.

Culture shock hit the hardest when I was deprived of daily comforts that made me feel all was well with the world. Like wiping my mouth without adding shredded paper to my meal.

What did the locals use? I pondered, still searching in vain.

I had seen some keep a roll of toilet paper on their table, ripping off strips as needed. It was hard to get past associating toilet paper with its original purpose.

Once in a while, I stumbled upon actual paper napkins. Inwardly, I danced a jig and bought as many packages as I could carry. *Who knows when the store will stock them again?* With each wipe of my mouth, I was thankful for one of those little niceties we take for granted back home.

My philosophical musing about the scant history of napkins in East Asia was interrupted by a need to visit the restroom.

There, I was starkly reminded of another important cultural difference. Their vast assortment of paper products were all kept on the store shelves, never in the stalls. I made a note to load another packet of tissues into my purse before going to the store again.

It's easy to think our way of doing things is the only way, or the best way. That applies not only to other cultures but also with respect to God.

Sometimes He wants us to look at something familiar in a new way. Like the way we use our free time, or our work and sleep schedule. He may want to replace an old habit with a new one.

When we pile up our familiar ways like walls of a fortress surrounding us, there's no room for anything new to come in or old to go out. Being willing to flex the way we view our small everyday routines and the objects involved may be uncomfortable at first. But it keeps us from hardening into inflexible concrete and prepares us for a new adventure ahead.

Reflect:
How do you view inconveniences in daily life?

Consider:
"For our light and momentary troubles are achieving for us an eternal glory that far outweighs them all."

— 2 Corinthians 4:17 NIV

What "light and momentary troubles" are you dealing with that don't feel momentary or light? How could this verse help you view them differently?

CHAPTER 25

Overseas Too Long?

Life overseas held its challenges, but one of the perks was vacations in nearby Thailand. The friendly hospitality and laid back atmosphere were always just what we needed. At the top of the list of activities I looked forward to were the massages at bargain basement prices.

One particular visit lived up to my expectations. Afterward, I walked slowly down the dim candle-lit hallway as a relaxing aroma wafted into my nostrils. Every detail from wallpaper to candles to gentle music was carefully planned to create a mood of luxurious tranquility. My two-hour-long massage unwound my muscles and mind, and I slowly approached the doorway that offered the final phase: herbal tea in the spa lounge.

Soft comfortable chairs beckoned me to lazily relax while sipping their exotic tea. I held my dainty cup under the electric water dispenser and pressed the hot water spigot.

Out gushed a clump of dead ants along with the water.

Without hesitation, I set that aside and poured a second cup, which was ant-free. I added the ginger tea mix and drank, casually completing my spa experience.

A few hours later, it suddenly hit me, with great alarm. *Did I really drink water that had ants boiling in it? Wow, maybe I've lived overseas too long.*

I didn't realize how much my environment was influencing me. I had changed on the inside and became more accepting (too accepting, in this case) of things I previously considered unwise. The boiled ants incident humored me, because in my younger years I was too cautious. I was no longer the same person. Sometimes change is good and frees us to step into new adventures; sometimes it limits how much we can enter into God's plan.

One basic characteristic of a living thing is that it grows. We are growing and changing, for good or for bad, whether we realize it or not. We constantly bump up against different values and perspectives. Many of them are "not wrong, just different," to quote our cross-cultural training instructor. Eating ants in some cultures is a delicacy, not a crime. I personally am not ready to go that far.

When you encounter a "boiled ants moment," you can ask God to reveal the inner attitudes and behaviors the event brought to the surface. Compare them to God's Word and character. If the Bible doesn't say one way or the other, you can consider it an opportunity to move into a different, but not wrong, adventure. If they reflect Him and His values, embrace the change. If the attitude or action is contrary to the Bible, He wants you to confess it and ask Him to change it.

Reflect:

Have you ever done something, then later you realized you acted or spoke before thinking about it?

Consider:

"And I am certain that God, who began the good work within you, will continue his work until it is finally finished on the day when Christ Jesus returns."

— Philippians 1:6 NLT

How have you been changed by the people or environment you live in? What choices can you make that will help you to be more influenced by godliness than ungodliness?

CHAPTER 26

When Your World is Shaken

"The flight is not even listed anymore! What do we do now?"

Our stomachs churned in alarm as we stared at the departure screen. We had moved to East Asia five months earlier but had flown to Orlando to celebrate our son's college graduation. Now we were returning to our new home overseas and had reached our second-to-last airport.

Exhausted from the long flight across the Pacific, we grew impatient as the last leg of our return was delayed several times. Now the flight details had disappeared from the overhead screen.

Our foreign language skills were minimal, but we were able to get our questions across to the airline clerk. She pointed to a word in a translation dictionary.

"Earthquake?" we read quizzically.

"*Little* earthquake," she clarified.

Nothing could have been a bigger understatement.

We soon learned that three hours earlier a massive 8.0 earthquake left a path of death and destruction an hour outside our new home. It demolished whole villages and killed over 87,000 people. Since everything was in chaos, including the airport, we would need to stay in this layover city.

We didn't know what we would face when we returned to our apartment two weeks later. Friends described how buildings swayed so violently that they could not grasp the handrailings for balance while running down the stairs. Thankfully, our city was built on bedrock, which absorbed much of the tremor's impact so few buildings were damaged.

But people's sense of security crumbled into a heap. Everywhere we looked, faces displayed the emotional aftershocks. For months, a common question people asked was, "Where were you when the earthquake hit?"

We grieved over the horrific losses that villages close to the epicenter experienced, and we did all we could to join the relief efforts. I almost felt guilty about the way God had spared my family from this disaster.

First, we missed the trauma of experiencing this earthquake firsthand because, at the last minute, we extended our time in Florida so we could be home for our younger son's 19th birthday.

Second, of all the Asian layover cities we could have landed in, this was the only one where we had good friends. God arranged a safe, comfortable place for us to stay until our city recovered enough for us to return.

Most of my most meaningful adventures spring up when I follow where Jesus leads me. If you and I place ourselves in God's Hands, nothing happens, good or bad, unless He allows it to pass through His protective grip.

Reflect:

Has there been a time when something you thought was solid, such as a business deal, a relationship, or the floor underneath you, was suddenly shaken? How did you react?

Consider:

"Those who live in the shelter of the Most High will find rest in the shadow of the Almighty. This I declare about the LORD: He alone is my refuge, my place of safety; He is my God, and I trust Him."

— Psalm 91:1, 2 NLT

Based on these verses, can you give Jesus permission to lead you into whatever He has planned for you, trusting He will be with you if something unexpected happens?

CHAPTER 27

On Christ the Solid Rock I Stand

When things were stable enough to return to our city, "life as usual" no longer existed. Physical and emotional aftershocks rocked our community several times a day. Long cracks in the hallway and our daughter's bedroom remained as evidence of the tumultuous shaking we had narrowly missed. Peter and I felt relieved when the inspector determined these deep lines didn't compromise the structural stability.

It was so good to finally unpack and settle into familiar beds that first night. But this celebration was short-lived. An urgent call shortly before midnight sent us scurrying into the night because experts predicted a large (6.0 to 7.0) aftershock. Friends advised us to evacuate our sixth-floor apartment and sleep at our friends' first-floor home, where we could exit quickly if necessary.

It was after midnight when we zig-zagged through the crowds blanketing the concrete park near our apartment. Fears that another big tremor would cause the apartment buildings to collapse brought most of the neighborhood outside in search of a safe place to spend the night.

Gone were the usual kites and skateboarders. Gone was the lively music blasting as couples waltzed away the day's stresses. These symbols of normal life had been replaced by hundreds of tents, cars transformed into living quarters, and handmade shelters of every shape and color.

We lugged overnight bags and gingerly tip-toed through the tangled mass of blankets and people. Dazed crowds slept anywhere there was a spot flat enough to lie down. I envied the togetherness and community our neighbors seemed to be experiencing as they gathered strength from each other's presence.

Mothers cradled their infants, bundling them up as if a blanket would offer protection from a collapsing structure. Children played tag with carefree abandon, innocently unaware of the seriousness of the occasion. Young couples huddled close, staring into each other's eyes with resolve to face whatever came. The unashamed and the exhausted slept soundly on their blankets in spite of the constant stream of displaced people passing by them.

The feared aftershock never came, but this episode was a powerful lesson in living the great adventure. When you and I follow the Lord of Life through the death of our own plans, He creates a new set better than our own.

My to-do list was replaced by a special bonding time with the family who hosted us that night, singing hymns around the piano. It also led to a meaningful conversation with a new friend who lived in their complex. I shared with her about an unshakable faith, which took root and blossomed in her life several years later.

The next day, I stood on the sidewalk among the locals and participated in their three minutes of silence to honor the dead. Tears rolled down my face as my sorrow mingled with theirs, and I felt strangely like one of them. Shared tragedy crumbles divisive walls as nothing else can. It joins us with others who are experiencing pain, too, and reminds us that we all need the Man of Sorrows acquainted with grief (Isaiah 53:3).

Reflect:
What deep loss have you experienced? How does it impact your relationship with others who have experienced something similar?

Consider:
"I am leaving you with a gift—peace of mind and heart. And the peace I give is a gift the world cannot give. So don't be troubled or afraid."
— *John 14:27 NLT*

Would your life be any different if you really believed Jesus is a solid Rock when life is shaking?

CHAPTER 28

Lessons Learned from the Earthquake Village

Crowds trudged toward us on the dusty road that wound between cornfields, emerging from makeshift tents and piles of bricks that seemed unlivable. Towering through the mist behind them was a mountain with the side sliced off. It was a stark reminder of the recent earthquake-caused landslide that buried everything in its path.

As we distributed cooking oil and rice to survivors, I had no idea I would receive much more than I gave that day. The adventure of entering someone else's world can bring startling clarity about what is really important in life. It helps you and me evaluate our worldview and priorities.

Many of these villagers had lost their homes. Most lost at least one person close to them. I learned important lessons that humbled me and challenged my level of comfort and convenience.

- If you lose everything you own, it doesn't mean you've lost everything of importance.

- A life lost can never be replaced, especially an only child.
- Bundles of corn stalks make great walls for a makeshift shelter.
- A bottle of cooking oil is the way to a woman's heart.

One woman warmly welcomed us into her tiny shack, which had somehow survived the tremors. A rough wooden table and two small stools leaned against one side, opposite an open firepit with a large wok. Walls made of coarse wood and unpainted concrete provided protection. There was no electricity, so there were no lamps. There were no decorative photos, but they had designed the floor in the beautiful earthy color of packed dirt.

She invited us to sit—actually squat— on tiny stools as she offered to feed us from the little she had. I learned several things from this simple, generous woman.

- You can be content with two wooden stools and a small handmade table, as long as you have a roof and walls, a cooking fire, a pot, and a smooth dirt floor.
- A hole next to the indoor pig pen works as a toilet even if you don't have fancy hand soaps and matching towels.
- No matter how little food you have, you have enough to share with visitors.
- No matter how busy you are, you always have time to welcome a stranger.

When curious children with dirt-smudged faces showed up at the woman's doorway, we taught them how to play Uno. It was especially rewarding to see them smile, knowing they had experienced far more death and loss than a child should have to process.

School had been in session when the earthquake struck. School buildings collapsed, claiming the lives of thousands of children from one-child families. How many of these young ones in front of us had been pulled out of the rubble, with their best friend lifeless beside them? We learned from the children, too.

- A jump rope provides hours of fun.
- An Uno game knows no language barrier.
- A new backpack is the way to a young boy's heart.
- If there is clear space in crumbled ruins, children will invent games they can play there.

At the end of the day, we gathered our volunteer group and piled onto the bus, waving to the grateful faces who were now friends. As we drove away, this adventure left me a different person than I was when we arrived.

- Laughter is an important ingredient of life, especially in a disaster.
- A smile speaks any language.
- When your village collapses, work together to rebuild it. Even if you only have bare hands and determination, you will succeed.

Reflect:

When have you entered into someone else's pain? How did it stretch you outside your comfort zone?

Consider:

"I know how to live on almost nothing or with everything. I have learned the secret of living in every situation, whether it is with a full stomach or empty, with plenty or little. For I can do everything through Christ, who gives me strength."

— Philippians 4:12, 13 NLT

How could you come alongside someone in need? Could you welcome a newcomer to your neighborhood? Or go on a mission trip?

Have You Embraced an Earthquake this Week?

The Bible says God has not even one speck of darkness/evil in Him (1 John 1:5) and that He is the personification of love (1 John 4:8-10). The adventures He allows are not to harm His children but to make our lives more meaningful.

There are countless opportunities to embrace a little more of life's "spice." They arrive in a variety of packages and often can enrich or lives once we get past our fears. Sometimes we need to believe by faith that God can bring good out of tragedy, like the earthquake aftermath.

Some of the young professionals who joined Peter and me to do relief work became close friends. Peter and I were more grateful and humbled after coming alongside those who live differently than we do. This was an adventure with a much deeper impact than riding through the backyard of a Buddhist monk compound.

Pray:

Lord, thank you that nothing surprises You. In Your love and wisdom, You allow a variety of events in my life. Help me to move forward and hold my plans loosely, knowing You may have something else in mind. Remind me to embrace it all, the good and the bad.

I have so much to learn from others! It's easy to think my way is best or even the only way to see things. I know that stepping into a new adventure may disrupt the way I have always done things, whether it's a new job or a new country. I give you permission to expand my borders and not allow me to be content within my comfort zone. In the matchless name of Jesus, amen.

SECTION FOUR

ENJOY!

Adventure comes in all shapes and sizes, but I never expected it would come shaped like a camel.

Our Israel tour group was tracing the life of Jesus, but Peter and I decided to sit out the strenuous hike on the edge of the desert. I couldn't picture the story ending well if I attempted to climb the rope ladder up the side of the cliff.

It's wise when choosing adventure to evaluate the risk compared to the gain. I decided I had more to gain by browsing in the mall next to the parking lot while those who went on the hike wondered why they did.

As we waited for the group to return, a man walked up and asked if we wanted a photo with his camel. I suspected something was up when I saw the man's mischievous smile. Just as the photo was snapped, his well-trained camel turned and planted a sloppy kiss.

CHAPTER 29

Paradise With My Fifty Close Friends

It could have been a Kentucky Fried Chicken convention at the Thailand train station.

Fried chicken cartons and the mountain of luggage grew by the minute. Boxes of Dunkin' Donuts were soon added to the jumble of backpacks and belongings as children of all ages ran excitedly to meet their friends. Adults hugged their greetings and looked expectantly for the train's arrival. Peter, our ten-year-old daughter, and I found our place in line. I watched in wonder.

It was a dream come true.

I had always wanted to vacation with friends but never imagined it being with this many. I didn't expect God would add fun surprises when we followed His call to East Asia. Now, only three weeks after arriving there, we had joined our new friends and coworkers in another country for the winter break.

The train pulled up, and our group, ages seven months to sixty years, filled a whole train car. A party on wheels.

After a few hours of bump-bumping past tin-roofed huts and rubber trees, the smell of fried chicken filled the air. It was dinner time.

The donuts were reserved for breakfast the following day, although a few were secretly sampled. These were special treats not found in the country we all served in and added to the celebratory atmosphere.

We each claimed top or bottom in the hallway stretch of bunk beds as the train lurched forward. I tried not to notice the roach skittering into the corner, or to wonder who slept last on my thin, bare mattress. Adapting to this "new normal" was part of the adventure.

Preteens and teens took their places at the tables at the end of the train car and began a marathon card game session. Judging by the frequent muffled laughter, it lasted far into the night. My heart was grateful that our daughter could enjoy such a unique experience.

One fitful sleep and a donut breakfast later, we arrived near the coast the following morning. Vans carried us another two hours until, finally, we saw the sun glimmering off of boats that would carry us to our destination. Our motley group skidded past unique rock formations until the boats pulled up near our isolated island in the middle of the Andaman Sea.

We rolled up our pant legs, took off our shoes, and gingerly stepped over the ledge of the boat to walk through the last twenty yards of knee-deep, crystal-clear water. Through the gentle waves, Thai sailors carried luggage after luggage on their shoulders and piled them on the sand.

My adventure cup was already full.

I gazed upwards at our hotel stretching up the side of the mountain with hundreds of stairs leading to various floors and the pool at the top. I breathed overwhelming gratitude that my compassionate Heavenly Father had healed our daughter's serious leg complication only a week earlier, making it now possible for her to lay aside her crutches and climb all these stairs.

What a wonderful time of rest. The lounge overlooking the ocean was always filled with meaningful conversation, card games, or square dancing. Sunrises were spectacular. God is a God who loves for us to enjoy the life He's given us and usually has a few surprises up His sleeve.

No time on a tropical island is without elements of danger that make for a great story. Like the cobra crossing the driveway. A worker caught it and carried it to his grass hut for dinner. Or poisonous sea urchins we had to snorkel cautiously around if we didn't want their toxic barbs stuck in our skin. Deceptively strong currents on our snorkeling excursion caught us off guard, along with the three-foot-long monitor lizards on the island where we ate a picnic lunch.

One activity best represented why we were there with fifty of our close friends. It took place on Sunday morning around the pool. Our singing floated down from the mountaintop as we drank in a beautiful panorama of tropical greenery. The sunlight sparkled off the blue-green ocean like a million white Christmas lights, with ruggedly shaped mountains shadowy in the distance. It was breathtaking and evoked a response of awe and gratefulness as our group held an informal worship service.

No noise of cars and buses, no hustle and bustle of masses of people, no air pollution, no hidden cameras and mics, no high-rise apartments blocking the colorful sunrise or sunset. I suspect that Jesus had gatherings like this in mind when he spoke this lush paradise into existence.

What had I done to deserve seeing such an amazing display of God's beauty? Nothing but follow Him and allow Him to adopt me as His beloved daughter.

"Then sings my soul, my Savior God to Thee –
How great thou art, how great thou art;
Then sings my soul, my Savior God to Thee –
How great Thou art! How great Thou art!"[2]

Reflect:

Would going on vacation with this many people be a blessing or a challenge for you? Why?

---

2 Boberg, Carl. "How Great Thou Art." Public domain, 1885.

Consider:

"Whatever is good and perfect is a gift coming down to us from God our Father, who created all the lights in the heavens..."

— James 1:17 NLT

What does this verse tell you about God's giving heart and the kinds of adventures He wants to give you?

CHAPTER 30

PETER, THE MODEL HUSBAND

I looked up and saw my husband Peter.

Oh, and there was Peter to the left.

And over to the right, was Peter also.

Like the oversized posters of a teenage heartthrob, Peter's picture was plastered on every inch of wall and pillar in the men's section of this high-end clothing store.

I'm not sure whose faces showed more surprise and amazement, Peter's, mine, or the store clerks who now stood face to face with the mysterious stranger they stared at every day.

It started with a friend of a friend's assignment to make her company's Asian-style dinner jackets appealing to foreigners. What could better accomplish this than using a foreign model? So our friend asked Peter.

I should mention that Peter hates trying on clothes. In fact, I buy most of his clothes. But to help our friend, he agreed. Peter spent eight tortuous hours trying on and posing for photos of every imaginable style of Asian jacket, with only minutes to jump into the next garment. He could almost see his breath in the cold changing room, which offered more motivation for him to grab the next outfit quickly.

The results of this photoshoot were completely unexpected. They printed a beautiful 40-page sales catalog of their men's product line. Every page had one thing in common: Peter.

Peter, who is most comfortable serving behind the scenes, became a celebrity. He was hailed as the "wallpaper of choice" at the clothing store. When American friends visited, this was their favorite part of our city tour. Inevitably, they took one look at the walls and burst into laughter. I wondered what the store clerks thought of that.

Living in another country presented many unexpected opportunities just because we were foreigners. God has a sense of humor. Life with Him is never boring! He has a way of using unlikely things to further His Kingdom. Peter's one-day modeling career opened new friendships with locals. When we showed them pictures of him wearing their customary clothing, they felt accepted and connected.

When you think you have seen it all, God surprises you with something else. Like our final visit to the classical clothing store before we moved back to the USA.

His picture was still plastered on the walls, but there was a new addition. A large computer screen continuously rotated photos of world leaders wearing the company's luxurious jackets: the president of the United States, the president of Russia, the president of China, the kings of other nations, and Peter.

Peter?

Yes, Peter.

When you climb into God's wagon, you had better expect the unexpected!

It might be scary, it might be exciting, or it might reflect God's humor, but will not be boring. He will probably take you out of your comfort zone, like trying on clothes is for Peter.

But He will always make it worth the ride.

Reflect:

Have you ever had something unexpected happen as a result of doing what you thought God wanted you to do?

Consider:

"You make known to me the path of life; you will fill me with joy in your presence, with eternal pleasures at your right hand."

— Psalm 16:11 NIV

What does this verse say to you? How does it encourage you to believe God will show you a meaningful path of life with unexpected enjoyment, if you follow Him?

CHAPTER 31

Frantic Night, Silent Night

I'm already late!

My stomach tightened two notches tighter as the traffic jam snaked around the corner. This was not the way to prepare to direct the Christmas play practice for my friend's school. She was counting on me, and so were her students. Nonetheless, traffic inched along while the taxi driver put me on edge with his reckless weaving in and out of the chaotic tangle of vehicles.

My mind wrestled with a jumbled mess of its own. Concerning thoughts honked and jostled for first place along my mind's highway. Urgent phone calls and emails I needed to make. The successful but exhausting Christmas party the night before. Grief over family holiday traditions we would miss celebrating with our grown children now that we lived halfway around the world. All I felt like doing was returning to our quiet apartment, burying myself in a soft blanket, and collapsing into a blob of nothingness.

I rushed up the elevator 15 minutes late with my festive spirit trailing several blocks behind. As I opened the school door, a soothing sound floated through the air and stopped me in my tracks. Where were those lilting voices singing "Silent Night" coming from?

It was twenty Asian students preparing for my arrival.

The Christmas story and our familiar carols were new to them. This performance was a creative way to share the greatest news on earth while developing their English skills. And since parents proudly show up any time their children perform, they, too, would hear about the best Christmas gift.

The young vocalists applauded wildly when they saw me and pleaded with me to sing "Silent Night." They wanted to know what it was supposed to sound like.

Do they have any idea how ill-prepared I am for their request?

I prayed for help while my friend fitted me with a microphone. As I softly sang that beautiful carol, it tenderly ushered me into a world without taxis, phone calls, or frantic lifestyles. A world where the dark night sky created a blanket of stillness as a new mother rested, in awe as she gazed at the sleeping face of God-in-the-Flesh. My heart was deeply touched by the wonder of what it would have been like to see the Glory of the Lord shining out of a helpless baby.

Peace flooded my soul as the verses flowed from my mouth. What an amazing event, that even the angels appeared in record numbers to herald His arrival! The King of Kings brought His Light into our darkness. He lavished on us His supreme offering so that we—and each one of these students before me—could experience His grace and redemption.

"I feel so peaceful when you sing!" my friend remarked after practice. In a way only God could orchestrate, my festive spirit caught up with me. He ministered deeply to me while I ministered to others.

The blanket of peace I experienced that night was deeper, more meaningful, and longer lasting than any soft blanket at home. He gave me what I needed the most: the simple eternal message of that first Christmas.

"Silent night, Holy night
All is calm, all is bright.
Round yon virgin, mother and child
Holy infant, tender and mild
Sleep in heavenly peace,
Sleep in heavenly peace."[3]

Reflect:
Where do you look for joy and peace?

Consider:
"But the angel said to them, 'Do not be afraid. I bring you good news that will cause great joy for all the people. Today in the town of David a Savior has been born to you; he is the Messiah, the Lord.' "

— Luke 2:10 NIV

How could the angel's timeless news give you peace and joy in stressful situations?

3 Mohr, Joseph. "Silent Night." Public domain,1818.

CHAPTER 32

Is That Mary Wearing My Tablecloth?

Seven shepherd costumes, three angel gowns, a few crowns...but where were Mary and Joseph's outfits? And the wise men and narrators' robes?

I knew it was risky waiting until the day before the play to pick up the costumes. Now my worst fears were realized. I could picture the parents glancing at each other disapprovingly, wondering why we bothered to put on such a slipshod program. Even worse, I felt sad at the thought of reenacting the greatest birth in history in a manner unworthy of the King of Kings.

I quickly cut my yards of shiny green fabric into simple wise man outfits, their rough unsewn edges tucked under so they were not obvious from a distance. But I needed more. Where could I find fabric for the two main characters' robes and head scarves for several others?

Lord, I need your help! Help me think outside the box!

Suddenly, I remembered my drawer full of tablecloths. I had

quite a collection since I love how they change the mood of a meal. Buried at the bottom was a beautiful blue-green cloth perfect for Mary's outfit. I added to the pile my scarves that had hung in the closet since receiving them for my birthday. We completed our nativity wardrobe with several other tablecloths, held in place by a few safety pins and strips of cloth. I enjoy the challenge and adventure of finding creative ways to improvise.

The dressing room filled with giggles and self-conscious looks as girls rearranged each other's scarves and nervously put hair strands in place. I was proud and relieved that the silliness stopped when the play began. Other than multi-colored sneakers sticking out below, you might think these school children were teleported from Bethlehem of long ago.

Our stage required a lot of the audience's imagination. The narrator's neatly arranged tablecloths shifted as the play went on, taking on the disheveled appearance of an ancient traveler. But the other costumes stayed in place, and the students beautifully reenacted this glorious event.

Parents excitedly videotaped and smiled, capturing this magical evening when ordinary tablecloths were transformed into something far more significant than holding stir-fried vegetables.

But more importantly, those parents and students who had never heard the Christmas story before can watch over and over again how an extraordinary God clothed Himself in ordinary flesh so that we can be transformed and take part in something far more significant than wearing tablecloths.

And that's what Christmas is all about, Charlie Brown.

Reflect:

Describe a time you did something in a new, creative way that's not limited by rules or tradition.

Consider:

"Now to Him who is able to do immeasurably more than all we ask or imagine, according to His power that is at work within us, to Him be glory in the church and in Christ Jesus throughout all generations, forever and ever! Amen."

— *Ephesians 3:20,21 NIV*

How does the world around us reflect God's immeasurable creativity and power? Is there a problem for which you could ask God to help you find a creative solution?

CHAPTER 33

Someone is Always Watching

"I'm at the fruit market," my daughter texted me. "You should be able to see me in a minute." I hurried to our sixth-floor balcony that faced the busy intersection she would be walking along and soon saw her familiar red sweater. As she looked up and noticed me, I decided to have a little fun, high above the hustle and bustle below.

So I waved my arms around, danced a little, and performed other crazy antics I am prone to do from time to time. *Of course, no one else would be looking up at our balcony,* I assured myself. Our daughter returned the crazy greeting from the sidewalk and soon was out of sight as she headed up the stairs to our apartment.

Peter arrived home a few minutes later and told us the rest of the story. He had taken a taxi home and, practicing his language skills as usual, made conversation with the driver.

"That's my apartment up there," he told the man. "Oh, and that's my wife on the balcony!"

At that point, I began dancing and acting crazy. Embarrassed, he tried to distract the smiling driver by pointing out our daughter walking along, right as she returned my unusual greeting. The driver may have wondered if this is what Americans do when they greet each other. I imagine he had an interesting story to tell at the dinner table that night.

We enjoyed a good laugh, especially when our friend later commented, "In this country, you can always assume someone is watching." It was true. Cameras and microphones were a way of life.

It reminded me that Someone Else is always watching, too.

God sees every action and hears every word. Psalm 139:1-3 says He knows what we are going to do even before we do it. Nothing escapes His notice.

He sees you give an anonymous gift to someone in need. He sees you sacrificially get up to feed the baby or comfort a sick child. He sees you faithfully heading to work every day when no one remembers to thank you. He hears the unkind words someone hurled at you and the wound it left in your soul. He notices and smiles when you are His hands and feet to a needy world.

He sees the sin you thought was done in secret. He hears the hurtful insult you let slip out in anger. He knows everything deep in our hearts and minds, including the bad thoughts and attitudes that we are surprised at ourselves. He views it all with grief and mercy.

Remembering He is always watching reminds us that we are never alone in our sorrow, never forgotten in our well-doing, and never alone in our sin. We can freely share our private thoughts, attitudes, and actions with Him because He already knows them and loves us, no matter what.

Reflect:

Can you think of a time when you were embarrassed that someone saw or heard something you thought was private? What happened?

Consider:

"This High Priest of ours understands our weaknesses, for He faced all of the same testings we do, yet He did not sin So let us come boldly to the throne of our gracious God. There we will receive His mercy, and we will find grace to help us when we need it most."

— *Hebrews 4:15, 16 NLT*

How does Jesus respond to the things we are ashamed of? Is there anything you would like to confess and ask Him for help with, remembering that He sees and understands everything you are dealing with?

CHAPTER 34

Bride of Frankenstein

What could possibly go wrong with the simple task of trimming an inch of hair straight across the bottom?

I soon found out.

I gathered my courage and entered a beauty salon for my first-ever Asian hair "trim." The whole shop's personnel gathered around my chair, eying my light blonde locks as they carefully followed the shampooer's every move.

Ahhh, this is the life!

I was pleasantly surprised that a twenty-minute head massage was included in the already low price of $3.50 for shampoo, cut, and style. My bargain-minded heart thumped excitedly. The shampooer meticulously wrapped my head in a towel and triumphantly led me to the chair in front of the window. This was so everyone who passed by could see that a foreigner trusted this shop with her hair, and they could, too.

As the hair stylist proudly removed my towel in front of the mirror, a hopelessly matted mess of hair stared back. Asian hair tends to be naturally smooth, shiny, and unlikely to tangle. They don't need the same treatment my curly Caucasian hair requires in order to avoid the my-head-got-caught-in-a-dog-fight look. That was when I painfully discovered that a head massage without hair conditioner not only relaxes the scalp, but also tangles wavy hair beyond recognition.

There I was. The Bride of Frankenstein. This was one of those times when a sense of humor comes in handy. I felt both sympathy and amusement when I observed the workers trying, unsuccessfully, to conceal their panicked faces. It seemed like they were thinking, *We destroyed the foreigner's hair! But we mustn't let her know we know.*

The stylist began gingerly running his comb through my hair, hoping for a miracle. Using my limited language, I said their word for "Trouble!" They quickly agreed and allowed me to comb it out myself. With each sweep of the comb I mentally prepared myself for the possibility that the final outcome might resemble the witch's broom in the Wizard of Oz. I wondered if this was the kind of front-window publicity they were hoping for.

Surprisingly, the snarls came out with minimal hair loss. The stylist proceeded to cut my hair with the utmost precision, impressing the audience which had grown larger by now. When he unveiled the final product, I breathed a huge sigh of relief. It actually looked good. One of the workers asked wistfully in broken English, "May *I* cut your hair *next* time?" I felt like a movie star being asked for a lock of hair.

I must admit, my self-image felt pretty good. All eyes watched me head out the door as they waved and gazed at my freshly trimmed tresses. I smiled as I thought about how so many common, everyday activities become adventures of faith when you live overseas.

Perhaps this experience was a little like life. Some challenges look like an impossibly tangled mess when we stare at the whole thing all at once. But if we take things slower and focus on a few strands at a time, the Master Hairstylist can not only get rid of the tangles but even make something nice out of it.

I decided to give the other hairstylist the thrill of cutting my hair next time.

But I skipped the head massage.

Reflect:
Is there anything new you have not tried because you fear the outcome?

Consider:
"And the very hairs on your head are all numbered. So don't be afraid; you are more valuable to God than a whole flock of sparrows."

— Luke 12:7 NLT

If you knew that God sees and cares about every detail, even bad haircuts, would you feel free to try something new and laugh if things didn't go the way you expected?

CHAPTER 35

THE MARKET

The marketplace felt like a step back in time.

I never lost my fascination with wandering through the traditional sights and sounds across the street from our overseas apartment. It was a wonderfully unique cultural experience.

Huge slabs of beef and plucked chickens dangled from meat hooks, as the overpowering smell of pungent spices wafted through the stale air. Loose eggs and basins of splashing fish waited to be chosen for dinner.

Stalls selling fabric, plastic bins, and dishware sat jumbled together alongside neat rows of vegetables or fruits and barrels of various kinds of rice. Vendors shouted their wares over the dull roar of humanity haggling for lower prices or sharing the latest gossip.

Imagine my disappointment when ambitious businessmen decided to demolish tradition to make room for the new. They tore down this market to build a multilevel shopping mall.

The old-style vendors and pleasantly chaotic blend of sights, smells, and sounds disappeared. The spot where neighbors once gathered now housed an impressively large—and empty— foyer with massive chandeliers. Its escalators led to five floors of 18 restaurants, 10 high-end stores, and a modern supermarket. Other than the Asian lettering on the walls, you would swear you were in America.

Each time we ventured into the mall for a meal, a few more restaurants were closed. Eventually, there were so few to choose from that we stopped going. Several months later, I just happened to peek into the mall entrance and was stunned.

Just below the foyer's sparkling chandeliers, pajama-clad housewives haggled with wrinkle-faced farmers as they tended their neat rows of fruits and vegetables. The huge stately foyer was now stacked wall to wall with the old market.

The pungent smell of local spices and pickled eggs permeated the air. Red slabs of meat and whole chickens hung from hooks, defying the USDA's warnings about meat left at room temperature. Barrels of tofu and rice settled nicely along the wall, just under the picture window where an expensive women's fashion store had been. The escalator leading to where the modern supermarket used to be was chained off. Everyone was happy again—except the unwise developers who tore down the market in the first place.

When we embark on an adventure that intersects with different people and cultures, we may be tempted to think our way is superior. The Lord didn't make us all the same, so He can show distinct aspects of His character through various cultures. His Word and His character remain the same worldwide, but how it is reflected may look different. Discover and respect Jesus' values and character in the world around you.

You can remove the people from the market, but you can't remove the market from the people.

Reflect:

What might this story show about understanding and valuing other cultures?

Consider:

"After this I saw a vast crowd, too great to count, from every nation and tribe and people and language, standing in front of the throne and before the Lamb. They were clothed in white robes and held palm branches in their hands. And they were shouting with a great roar, 'Salvation comes from our God who sits on the throne and from the Lamb!'"

— *Revelation 3:9-10 NLT*

Every Christian from every nation will be together in Heaven, worshipping Him. Do you know a Christian from a different culture? Could you spend time with them this week?

CHAPTER 36

God Works at Starbucks

"Are you a student?"

My concentration was unexpectedly disturbed by a smiling face staring down at me. I nodded yes, but it seemed like an odd question. Most people I know don't study language textbooks for fun while sipping coffee at Starbucks.

But it was her next comment that threw me.

"So sorry I'm late!" she exclaimed, as she enthusiastically plopped down across from me.

Late?? I have never seen this woman before in my life. Or have I?

I didn't want to embarrass both of us by admitting I had no idea who she was, so I fished around for clues as we casually talked. I began to suspect God was up to something when she pulled out two thick books and mentioned she was looking forward to studying the Bible together.

Soon the mystery was solved. She had not asked me, "Are you a student?" She had asked me, "Are you Susan?" Tina had been reading the Bible but didn't understand it. Her friend suggested she meet with Susan, who could explain it to her. Susan, I believe by God's arrangement, was late. I was the only foreigner sitting in Starbucks so Tina assumed I was Susan.

Susan finally arrived. Tina and I agreed it seemed like God had arranged our meeting, so when we said goodbye I invited her to my apartment the following week.

All week long, I puzzled, *Why did the Lord put me in Tina's life when she already had Susan to teach her the Bible?* When Tina and I finally met, I shared how to become a Christian and she asked Jesus into her life.

Then Tina showed me the Bible Susan gave her. It was an inaccurate translation used by a cult! Now it all made sense. God had seen Tina's seeking heart and channeled her away from false teaching so she could come to know Him. I had the incredible adventure of being His instrument to guide her to Himself.

A couple weeks earlier I read Acts chapter 8, where God led Philip to the Ethiopian eunuch who wanted to understand the Bible. I prayed in response, "Lord, in this city of 14 million people, surely there must be at least one person truly seeking to know You. Would You bring anyone like that across my path please?"

And He did.

Tina became my closest friend and disciple. I watched her life change before my eyes and she became co-leader of my Bible study, using her amazing translation skills as a bridge between the locals and me. She married an American who grew up in her country and combined their callings to reach an unreached people group high up in the mountains. Her desire, she says, is to pour herself into others like I poured my life into hers.

By far, the greatest and most rewarding adventures I have experienced have been when God has invited me out of my little world and allowed me to help carry out His eternal purposes. Joining His work of reconciling others to Himself is an adventure like no other. Hands down.

What I would have missed out on if I had not misunderstood Tina's question that memorable autumn day! Would I have met her at all if I had not made myself available for the Lord to use me?

Jesus delights in giving us the privilege of front-row seats to watch as He changes lives and then uses those lives to impact other lives. Sometimes, we get so distracted by other things that we forget to pray the simple but powerful prayer, "Lord, use me today. Lead me to someone whose heart You have prepared."

It could be the neighbor who always jogs past your driveway. Or your child's classmate's parent. The crossing guard. The grocery store cashier.

Or the smiling face staring down at you in Starbucks.

Reflect:
Have you ever experienced an encounter you felt was arranged by God?

Consider:
"Therefore, we are ambassadors for Christ, as though God were making an appeal through us; we beg you on behalf of Christ, be reconciled to God."
— 2 Corinthians 5:20 NASB

What would it be like to be Jesus's ambassador to those around you?

CHAPTER 37

Body-less Heads and Re-Birthdays

A cart full of body-less heads?

That is what rolled past me as I turned to cross the street in East Asia.

I stole a second glance, relieved to discover they were mannequin heads from a clothing store renovation. I was already in a pensive mood since it was the 35th anniversary of the day I trusted Jesus to come into my life. My spiritual birthday. So it occurred to me that the fact God had chosen me to be His beloved daughter and sent me to live in East Asia was more amazing than a cart full of heads.

As I walked past now-familiar strange sights, my thoughts returned to that fateful day when my fiancé (not Peter) squirted me with a water hose. His response to my squirting him back was to race away and not call for three days.

The Lord used that painful event to open my eyes. Suddenly I realized that Jesus was the only One who loved me perfectly and was worthy of my trust. The next day—August 12, 1973—I went to church for the first time in years. Sitting alone, gazing up at the cross I prayed, "Lord, If you have a better plan than mine, I am interested. And if I can know you the way those two girls in college told me about, I want to."

I am filled with awe and gratitude for all He has done in me and through me since then. The Nancy of 52 years ago would be terrified by the everyday risks required to live in a foreign country. But here I am—living, breathing proof of His unfathomable grace and transformation.

What did He see in me back then as He drew me to Himself? I was just a young, confused girl who was willing to take that first small and uncertain step of faith which, at the time, seemed like as big of a leap as from there to Asia.

I can›t adequately express what it has been like to know Jesus and walk with Him for all these years.

Simply said:

- He is real.
- He loves me with overwhelming compassion.
- He delights in me simply because I am His own.
- He is God, and I am not.
- Nothing is too big for Him to handle, and nothing is too small for Him to care.
- He never changes.
- He knows best.
- Nothing surprises Him.
- He can always be trusted.
- He is my tender, compassionate Father whose shoulder is always available to cry on.

As I look back, I see His overwhelming faithfulness to gently, lovingly lead me one step at a time on the road He chose for me. He supplies whatever I need in order to accomplish every task He has called me to. In the process, He drew me closer to Himself. His greatest desire is not for me to do work for Him; it is for me to know and love Him.

Later, on my special day, we explained to a new believer and her boyfriend how to live the Christian life. Peter and I both became excited as we were reminded of these wonderful truths someone shared with us many years ago. As we encouraged them to follow God's plan for love and marriage, I sensed her increasing hunger to learn and grow.

Just like me, 52 years ago.

Reflect:

Was there a point in your life when you trusted Jesus to come into your life as your Savior? If so, what are you most grateful for?

Or, would you like to know how to receive Christ? If so, there's great news in the back of this book entitled "Have You Reserved Your Ticket?".

Consider:

"All praise to God, the Father of our Lord Jesus Christ, who has blessed us with every spiritual blessing in the heavenly realms because we are united with Christ. Even before he made the world, God loved us and chose us in Christ to be holy and without fault in his eyes."

— Ephesians 1:2,3 NLT

Take a few minutes to thank God for His blessings, spiritual and otherwise. Thank Him for the adventures He has planned for you.

Are You Enjoying Life's "Camel Kisses"?

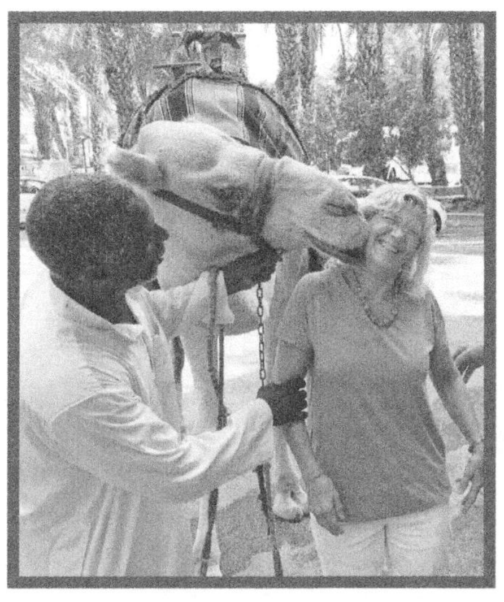

I love seeing and doing unique things, whether I am home carrying out my daily routine or touring the ancient ruins of Israel.

Have you ever been kissed by a camel? I hadn't. I avoided one adventure by skipping the hike where I would have fallen to my death from a rope ladder (okay, that's an exaggeration, but the struggle was real!), but the Lord was faithful to give me a never-before experience anyway.

The very nature of adventure is unexpected, unusual, and stretches you to somewhere you haven't been before. The more comfortable we become with not being comfortable, the more we can enjoy the surprises life brings us.

Suggested Prayer:

Thank you, Heavenly Father, for choosing to involve us in Your significant work. This is not because You need us to, but because You know we will be blessed by it. You are not hovering over us with a clipboard and furrowed brow, recording all our offenses. You love us! You delight in us as Your children. Remind me today and every day to look for the many big and little adventures You give me to enjoy. In Jesus' name, amen.

EPILOGUE

The Unlikely Adventurer Lives On

My stomach tightened, and I thought my heart would beat out of my chest. The intensity of my panic over this little detail caught me off guard. *I had successfully planned and executed so many trips before this one. What was the big deal?*

The next day, my sister Liz and I were flying nonstop from Orlando to Montreal, then taking the train to Quebec for our annual four-day sisters' getaway. I had researched everything thoroughly, mentally walking through the itinerary to be sure my plans went perfectly. I thought I had everything under control.

The only unknown was whether we could make it from the airport to the train station in time for the one o'clock train. Otherwise, we would have to wander around Montreal with our luggage for four hours until the five o'clock train.

After looking at maps, determining traffic, and considering a possible flight delay, I concluded, *I'm 95 percent certain we can make the one o'clock train. Yay! But not entirely certain. Of course, the train won't be full. We can just buy our tickets at the train station.*

But when I checked the train ticket website the night before, the unthinkable popped up on my screen: *sold out*. The one o'clock train was sold out!

My best-laid plans for a neat package tied together by the ribbon of my control unraveled. An avalanche of what-ifs jumped onto the loudspeaker of my mind and made sure I was rudely reminded of each one.

I told you I'm an unlikely adventurer, didn't I?

Even after wearing out the wheels on several suitcases and filling the pages of my passport, I easily default to depending on myself as my solid foundation instead of God. I still can cling to my illusion of being in control and then melt into a tizzy when that bubble bursts. I usually get butterflies a day or two before flying and have the worst time deciding what to wear on the plane. My compulsion to feel prepared for the unexpected makes it challenging to pack lightly. On this trip, I took a big step out of my comfort zone by packing just a carry-on bag.

On the night of my near-panic attack about the train, I had momentarily forgotten that God is God and I am not. He still held His hand firmly underneath me. He wasn't surprised or about to allow His firm foundation to crumble.

Jesus gently reminded me that He was going to Quebec with me. If I wanted to enjoy this adventure or any other adventure, I needed to let go of my effort to control everything and my fear of the unexpected. Only then could I embrace and enjoy a bigger, better story—His story—and trade my plans for His plans.

Liz and I had a wonderful trip. The savory seasoning of the unknown and unexpected added so much to our adventure. It made the difference between bland and lip-smacking memories.

Checking our luggage into the Montreal train station's convenient lockers (a pleasant surprise!) freed us to explore the area's fascinating maze of retail establishments. We wandered through so many cute shops, cafes, and cobblestone streets that we almost didn't notice the rain seeping into our socks and clothing. Sampling maple syrup delicacies was lip-smackingly wonderful. After several crazy photos in the old-fashioned telephone booth, it was time to head to Quebec.

My best-laid plans went smoothly. But I could never have arranged the experiences we will talk and laugh about for years to come.

We smile when we remember the castle tour guide, fully attired in early English costume, who shared little-known secrets about the founding father, Samuel de Champlain.

We were surprised by the city's stairs, stairs, and more stairs, but it made finding the funicular (similar to a cable car, but it goes down the mountain so you don't have to use the stairs) especially sweet. The creepy guy in the Airbnb, who was standing outside our door when I opened it, added unexpected drama. Best of all, my sister and I grew closer and pocketed new memories, even though she concluded our journey with a case of COVID-19.

Courage doesn't mean you never feel afraid; it just means that when fears show up, you put them in the backseat, not behind the steering wheel.

Imagine what I would have missed out on if I had allowed my fears to keep me from exploring new territory. As Jesus grows bigger in your life, the power of your fears grows smaller. The better you know Jesus and how good and trustworthy He is, the easier it is to let go of the things that hold you back and embrace whatever He wants to replace them with. When you know that the most important constants in your life will never change, you can enjoy the thrill of discovering new things.

I hope my stories have awakened a desire for something more, something that starts with the Great Adventurer. I hope you have decided it's worth the risk of breaking out of your comfortable cocoon so you can taste and experience a fuller life.

My prayer is that you have chosen to trust your ordinary life into the hands of the extraordinary God, who will lead you and provide what is necessary for your unique and incredible adventure.

Now, where do you want to go from here?

Bonus Features

Have You Reserved Your Ticket?

(Bible verses are NASB unless indicated otherwise)

You may have read my stories and thought, "I can't say that I know Jesus personally, the way Nancy talks about Him." Well, there's good news—you can know Him, too!

I would love to visit with you in person and introduce you to the trustworthy God I have come to know and love. I'd explain the Bible verses that have become dearer to me since I heard them many years ago.

But since we can't meet face to face, let's imagine we are sitting at my dining room table, and you just asked how you could know God personally and begin the great adventure He created you for. I sip my coffee, smile, and share the message I never grow tired of telling.

Jesus Loves You!

The first thing I say is, "Jesus loves you, just as you are. When I first heard this, it grabbed my attention. I don't always feel loved or lovable, yet the Bible says it's true.

"Jeremiah 31:3 says, 'I have loved you with an everlasting love; I have drawn you with unfailing kindness.'

"Isn't it amazing that God has loved you since before the world began, and is inviting you to know Him now? His actions have proved his words.

" The Bible says, 'God so loved the world that He gave His one and only Son, that whoever believes in Him shall not perish but have eternal life' (John 3:16).

"Not only that, but God also has a wonderful plan for your life, far better than you could come up with yourself. Jesus said, 'I came that they might have life, and might have it abundantly' (John 10:10). He wants to give each of us a life overflowing with meaningful purpose."

I smile and ask, "Did you know God loves you and created you for a special purpose?"

You might reply, "I never thought about it before."

But There's a Problem...

We move on to another question. "Why do you think most people are not experiencing the meaningful life Jesus promised?" I break off a small piece of my banana bread, pop it into my mouth. I nod as I listen to your response.

Then I gently explain that the Bible says it's because "All have sinned and fall short of the glory of God" (Romans 3:23).

You help yourself to another piece of banana bread, and I continue, "Sin means we have chosen to go our own way instead of God's. We want to be like God and control everything instead of trusting Him to be in charge. Before I met Jesus, I was a pretty good person. I never realized that just leaving God out of my life, except when I wanted Him to help me, was a sin. Sin involves both active rebellion and passive indifference, which separate us from God and His love."

When I first heard this, it didn't take long to think of things in my life that qualified as sin. Maybe you feel guilty as your past choices come to mind, too. Because God is perfect and holy, He can't allow one speck of sin in His presence. And there's no way we can ever be free from our self-centered motives.

The Bible says, "The wages of sin is death" (Romans 6:23). I explain to you that the word "death" means separation. Spiritual death means spiritual separation from God.

"Every person has a longing to know God, so we try to reach Him in our own way, like trying to follow the Ten Commandments, helping others, and exploring different philosophies. But there is nothing we can do to remove our sin or make ourselves good enough to please God."

You may feel a little hopeless at this point and wonder why I invited you over to tell you this

God Offers Us a Solution..

I lean forward excitedly because I am about to tell you something incredible. "Remember I told you there's good news? Well, there's a solution for the separation between us and God!"

Before I can continue, our tiny brown poodle puts her paws on your chair, looking for attention. She wags her tail hopefully, stares into your eyes, and assumes you came to see her. You pat her head and pick her up, and I continue.

"The Bible says, 'God demonstrates His own love toward us, in that while we were yet sinners, Christ died for us' (Romans 5:8). Jesus paid for our sins, so we no longer need to be separated from God and His love.

"Not only that, He rose from the dead!" I exclaim. " The Bible says, 'Christ died for our sins ... He was buried ... He was raised on the third day, according to the Scriptures ... He appeared to Peter, then to the twelve. After that, He appeared to more than five hundred' (1 Corinthians 15:3-6)."

You listen attentively, even if this is very new. Something inside of you might wonder, *Could this be the answer to the emptiness I feel inside?*

"Jesus said to him, 'I am the way, and the truth, and the life; no one comes to the Father, but through Me'(John 14:6).

"Jesus is the only person in history to offer a solution for our sin. God bridged the separation between Himself and us by sending His only Son, Jesus Christ, to die on the cross for our sins. But there's something we need to do to make His forgiveness ours."

By now, the plate of banana bread has only a few crumbs left, and you wait to hear how you can make God's forgiveness yours. This may be your first time hearing what the Bible says, or you may have heard it many times before, but there's something inside you that wants more. And I don't mean more banana bread.

An Important Decision!

We laugh as my dog paws at your leg, hoping you will pick her up again. This time, I find a bone for her and send her on her way before continuing to the next important point.

"Remember when I offered you banana bread? What did you need to do to make it your banana bread?" I ask.

"I needed to accept it. Otherwise, I would be sitting here hungry!" you reply, with the speed of a game show contestant.

"Exactly! It's the same way with God's gift. We must individually receive Jesus Christ as Savior and Lord to know and experience the great adventure He created us for. And you become His child! The Bible says, 'As many as received Him, to them He gave the right to become children of God, even to those who believe in His name' (John 1:12).

Knowing God is a free gift. "By grace you have been saved through faith; and that not of yourselves, it is the gift of God; not as a result of works, that no one should boast" (Ephesians 2:8-9).

"When I first heard this verse, it surprised me that I can do nothing to earn God's approval. God paid a very high price, the life of His only Son. When I began to understand these truths, I told God I wanted to receive His Gift. You can take that step of faith, too."

You interrupt me here. "Wait, are you saying that for all these years I have been trying to be good enough to please God, Jesus has been offering His forgiveness to me as a free gift?"

"Exactly!" I reply. "Not only that, if you invite Him into your life, He promises to come in and never leave. In Revelation 3:20, Jesus says, 'Behold, I stand at the door and knock; if anyone hears My voice and opens the door, I will come in to him.'

"It's kind of like this. When you knocked on my door, I had three choices. I could ignore you and hope you would go away; I could tell you to come another time; or I could open the door and welcome you in!"

"I'm happy you didn't tell me to go away when I knocked on your door!" you comment with a smile.

"I am happy I didn't either, because I am enjoying our visit!" I laugh, then go on.

"Jesus is knocking at the door of your life. Now that I've explained how you can know God personally through Jesus, you have three choices: ignore Him, tell Him you will consider it another time, or open the door.

"Receiving Christ involves deciding to do things God's way instead of your own (repentance), trusting Christ to come into your life to forgive your sins and make you the person He created you to be. To know in your head that Jesus Christ is the only Son of God and that He died on the cross for your sins is not enough. Nor is it enough to have an emotional experience. You receive Jesus Christ by faith, as an act of the will.

"I prayed a prayer like this many years ago when I became a Christian. If it expresses the desire of your heart, then you can pray this right now, and Christ will come into your life, as He promised:

"Lord Jesus, I want to know you personally and join Your great adventure. Thank you for the bridge you made between us when you died on the cross for my sins. I open the door of my life and receive You as my Savior and Lord. Thank You for forgiving me and giving me eternal life. Make me the kind of person You created me to be.

"Does this prayer express the desire of your heart?" I ask you. "If it does, you can pray it right now, and Jesus will come into your life as He promised."

What Just Happened?

Right there in the privacy of my dining room, you bow your head and quietly invite Jesus into your life.

Then an event of eternal importance takes place. You and I read what the Bible says just happened.

1. Jesus came into your life and will never leave you (Hebrews

13:5).

2. Your sins, past, present, and future, were removed as far as the East is from the West (Psalms 103:12).
3. You became a child of God, which means God is your perfect Father and you have a huge family, with other Christians as your brothers and sisters (John 1:12).
4. You can know for certain that you have eternal life (1 John 5:13).
5. You began the great adventure God created you for (John 10:10).

"Oh, I have just the thing!" I jump up and hurry into the kitchen. I return to the dining room with the rest of the banana bread, topped with a candle. We use it as your spiritual birthday cake to celebrate your spiritual birthday.

"Peter! Join us. Our friend just made the most important decision of their life!"

After Peter welcomes you into God's family, we light the candle, sing Happy Re-birthday to you, and then enjoy more banana bread. You may not feel any different, or you may feel a new peace and joy. The facts in the Bible about you and your new relationship with Jesus are always true. They don't depend on feelings.

"Don't forget today's date! It's your spiritual birthday," I warmly encourage you. We visit and laugh for a while; then, sadly, it's time to go.

"Would you like to meet again to discuss how you can grow to know Jesus better?" I ask, as you gather your jacket to leave.

"I'd love to!" you respond. "Since I am only visiting and return home tomorrow, could we text each other and do video calls?"

"That's a great idea! Let's be sure we have each other's contact information." My heart feels happy because I just had the incredible privilege of introducing you to the Great Adventurer.

Nothing Would Thrill Nancy More

Well, so much for my imagined visit with you. What was your response? We will probably never enjoy banana bread together at my dining room table, but there are other ways to be in touch.

Maybe you are already a Christian and have gained new encouragement in your faith and how to share it with others.

Maybe you prayed to ask Him into your life.

Maybe you want to know more.

Nothing would thrill me more than to hear your response to this imagined meeting and how this book touched your life. You can email me at **AdventureswithJesus2025@gmail.com.** I would love to hear from you.

I will sit at my dining room table to read it and reply. I might even eat banana bread while I respond!

Taking Off on Your Great Adventure

Find a Solid Foundation.

Discover the God who created you.
God, I want to know you. Please be my solid foundation and guide me to Your plan for my life. Help me to focus on how adequate You are, not on how uncertain I am.

Check off one action below that you will begin this week:

- ☐ Read the Bible daily, starting with the Gospel of John. Look for truths about what God is like and write them down.
- ☐ Observe, in the Bible and other Christians, God's heart to bring others to Himself.
- ☐ Join a small group Bible study where you can grow in your Christian life.
- ☐ Visit a church in your area that seems like you might feel at home in.
- ☐ Become part of a church family.
- ☐ Dream big! How could you be a part of God's plan?

Write your own prayer in response to this book:

Resources

- *JesusFilm* iPhone app
- *EveryStudent* app or everystudent.com
- *Cru* iPhone app
- *BibleHub* app

Release

Dear Jesus, help me to let go of.... (check the ***top three*** *that apply) so I can move forward into whatever adventure you have for me.*

- ☐ being in control
- ☐ Fear of danger and not being in control of my safety
- ☐ Fear of failure
- ☐ Fear of what others may think
- ☐ Pride
- ☐ Negative self-talk and past hurts that limit me
- ☐ The future (imagined fears)
- ☐ The security I find in things that are familiar and predictable
- ☐ Unrealistic expectations
- ☐ Expecting to do things perfectly when I attempt something new
- ☐ Wanting to know all the details before I take a step

Embrace

God, I receive by faith everything you allow to come my way. I want to follow You and Your plan because I know I can trust you even when it looks different than I expected.

Discover who He created you to be.

God, I want to know who you made me to be and what good works you have planned for me.

- ☐ Be a student of yourself. See what common threads these "puzzle pieces" contain.
- ☐ Take online career and personality tests. There are several, free and for purchase.
- ☐ Participate in The Significant Woman or Man of Impact, which involves life coaching and self-discovery.
- ☐ Take a "Spiritual Gifts" questionnaire and discover what yours is. How could you take a step forward in using it?

Gather more clues to who God created you to be and do. Are there some common themes in the answers?

- ☐ What do you do well?
- ☐ What do others say you do well? Ask three people who know you well.
- ☐ What gets you excited and grabs your heart?
- ☐ What were your dreams when you were young? Are they perhaps a window into your true heart?
- ☐ What needs in the world are you burdened by?
- ☐ What is your favorite part of your current job?
- ☐ What skills and training do you have? What might be the logical next step in developing and using them further or in a new way?
- ☐ What do your emotional wounds make you compassionate about?

What did you learn about yourself through your answers? What are the common themes?

____

____

____

____

Choose one or two from this list. Then fill in the two blanks at the bottom.

- ☐ Learn new ways to do old things.
- ☐ Go on a mission trip! It can be needed within your country, or somewhere far away.
- ☐ Become friends with at least one like-minded person or group who encourages you to have an adventurous spirit.
- ☐ Become friends with at least one person from a different culture.
- ☐ Develop a sense of humor, especially about yourself.
- ☐ Work on seeing a lack of success as a learning opportunity, not a failure.
- ☐ Ask questions! Ask more questions!
- ☐ Check into further training or education in a current skill, which will lead to new opportunities.

The next step outside my comfort zone is______________________ ______________________.

Something new I plan to try is______________________________ ______________________

Resources

- Free career, personality and IQ tests: **123test.com**
- Comprehensive career evaluation: **careerdirect.org**
- *The Significant Woman* and *Man of Impact*: **thesignificantproject.org**
- Spiritual Gifts survey: **gifts.churchgrowth.org/spiritual-gifts-survey**
- Tools and training to share your faith: **godtoolsapp.com**

Enjoy!

Lord of the Universe, thank you for placing so many interesting things around us! Remind me that the most interesting and meaningful experiences are often outside my comfort zone.

Learn from others.

Dear God, Help me to discover more about the world outside my comfort zone. I never want to stop learning! It's an adventure in itself.

- ☐ Read or listen to biographies of those who accomplished great things by taking risks and trying new things.
- ☐ Learn about different cultures, and the needs in those places. Could you help?
- ☐ Travel. Go with a tour group or mission trip, if you are not up to planning it yourself.
- ☐ Learn a new language and find someone nearby you can practice it on. Or better yet, visit where they speak that language.

Check two or three areas you want to grow in.

- ☐ Think BIG! "If I knew I couldn't fail, I would...." Complete this sentence. Then give it a try!
- ☐ Never stop learning.
- ☐ Travel. Then travel more, even if it's to a new restaurant on the other end of your city or town.
- ☐ Identify your limits, then intentionally move outside of them.
- ☐ Don't be too quick to say no. Evaluate why you said no without considering it more fully.
- ☐ Help others.
- ☐ Be God's ambassador, the most exciting adventure in the world!
- ☐ Keep physically active.
- ☐ Think outside the box.
- ☐ Be willing to pay the price, assuming it's worth the reward.
- ☐ Explore the adventure within You by having the courage to face difficult memories or wounds within

Resources:

There are endless Christian biographies available. Some of my favorites:

- Christian Heroes: Then and Now series by Janet Benge
- *Seven Men* and *Seven Women* by Eric Metaxas
- *Through Gates of Splendor* by Elizabeth Elliott
- *Bruchko* by Bruce Olson
- The Sower Series

The greatest adventure is wherever you are following the Great Adventurer and partnering in His big story!

PRACTICAL TRAVEL TIPS

Many of our adventures are in our own backyard! But if your great adventure leads you away from home, here are some travel tips that I've found helpful.

Planning:

1. Be well prepared. You will have unexpected things happen, and they may be your favorite part of the adventure. But to minimize unwanted surprises, take care of whatever you can ahead of time. Then you won't get as stressed by unexpected last-minute things.
2. Start with the big framework: dates that could work and your purpose(s). My favorite is to be part of a mission trip, then add a few days before or after to experience new sights. If you want ideas, feel free to email me!
3. Figure out your budget.
4. Find your passport and check that it is current. Check your destination's requirements well in advance so you have time to renew it if necessary. Most countries require at least six months left on your passport. If you need a visa, check out the turn-around time and get it started.
5. Buy your flights to and from. Check for the best prices, the most direct routes, or routes with an interesting layover. For example, Icelandair currently offers free layovers in Iceland.
6. Sometimes there's a flight with a long layover, like 12-20 hours. You could do a quick tour of another city besides your primary destination.
7. Draw or print a simple calendar of the dates of this adventure. Divide each day into three sections: morning, afternoon, and evening. Pencil the places you want to go on the calendar.

Don't forget to include travel time from place to place. This will help you see if it's realistic or not. Leave enough gaps in your itinerary so you are not too busy rushing from place to place to relax, enjoy the experience, or do something last-minute you discovered along the way.

8. Do you know anyone who lives at the location you are visiting? The ideal is to have someone local show you around. Ask them as many questions as you have about climate, money, favorite places, etc.
9. Is English commonly spoken where you want to go? If not, Google how other English speakers get around without knowing the language. Download a translation app, if needed.
10. Determine how you will travel while you are in a location. If driving sounds more stressful, especially on the other side of the road than you are used to, consider trains and the subway. They can be an adventure in themselves and add more opportunities to interact with locals. Buses are okay, too, but keep in mind they seldom have restrooms and you can't move around.
11. If you are considering public transportation, check out whether the particular stations and modes of transport are safe in that area. Check out if getting to the station from your lodging is easy. Find out whether taxis or Uber are available, and if the station is too far to walk to. Check the exact departure and arrival times to be sure you can get to the museum, etc., in the planned time.
12. Calling or emailing the front desk where you will be staying can be a great source of information, such as the questions in number 10 and 11.
13. If you are driving, check distances to be sure you are realistic about what you can fit in.
14. If you feel anxious about what kind of roads you must travel on, check Google Earth ahead of time. It is incredible what you can see.

15. For international trips, even to Canada, check with your phone service whether you have global coverage. If not, ask how to activate it during your trip.
16. Take paper maps as a backup plan. They also give you a bigger picture than GPS offers.
17. Take a photo of your luggage before checking it in at the airport. If it's lost, you have a description; and if it's damaged, you have a before photo to prove it was fine before.

Packing:

1. If you bring a travel pillow or blanket, be sure it's a brightly colored print so it doesn't blend in with hotel sheets and get left behind.
2. Bring an empty water bottle in your carry-on and fill it at the water fountain on the other side of security, to avoid paying extra for water close to your gate.
3. Bring your favorite teabag and place it in your filled cold water bottle. Tea will diffuse even if the water is not hot, and you will have flavored water for your flight.
4. Bring a sub, salad, or sandwich in your carry-on. You won't have to worry about having enough time to buy lunch or dinner during a short layover or pay high prices for a meal on the flight.
5. Use luggage cubes to organize clothes: roll them and store pants in one, tops in another, underwear/pajamas and socks in another, sweaters, swim, and exercise items in another. They are like portable drawers you can stack on a shelf wherever you are. You can see everything in each cube when rolled and stacked sideways. Some cubes compress, which makes excellent use of luggage space.
6. Organize snacks, medication, and vitamins in separate zipper bags. It's much easier to find things as you travel.
7. Save old prescription bottles for small amounts of shampoo, etc.
8. Disposable plastic shower caps make good shoe covers.

9. Double Ziploc bag anything that would be a mess if it broke into the rest of your suitcase.
10. Store small items in your packed shoes to save space and protect them from breaking.
11. If you carry books or papers in your luggage, put them in plastic bags. It can soak through even hard-sided luggage if it's raining when they take your bags off the plane.
12. Carry necessary medications and a change of clothes in your carry-on.
13. Small disposable toothbrushes prevent gritty teeth on long flights.
14. Carry a portable phone charger. Your phone is probably indispensable for your trip to go smoothly, and sometimes the battery wears down more quickly when you're using the roaming capacity.
15. Pack a small amount of fluoride mouth rinse or paste. If you develop a toothache, it can help reduce the pain.

If You are Flying:

1. When you reserve tickets, be sure you are given at least two hours between flights when you first land in the country you are going to (including coming home), so you have enough time to go through customs.
2. If you travel with someone, book the aisle and window seat. The middle seat may remain empty.
3. Book seats at the back of the plane for overnight flights. You are more likely to have empty seats next to you to lie on.
4. Seats in front of emergency exits and the last row usually don't recline, so avoid these if you need a reclining seat.
5. Seats behind the bathroom and galley don't have storage under the seat in front of you (because there is no seat in front of
6. you), but they may have extra legroom.
7. Email your reservations to someone else as a backup plan.

8. For me, it relieves stress when I have the details on paper and not just on my phone. Print tickets, hotel and car rental reservations, and sightseeing tickets. Number them in the order you will use them and organize them in a folder.
9. The Flight Aware app tells you where your airplane is coming from and when. If you know it's coming from bad weather, you can assume you may be delayed.
10. For most early flights, the plane came in the night before. So, early flights are less likely to be delayed than later ones.
11. Check online airport maps to figure out if you would be able to get from your arrival gate to your departure gate for a tight layover.

On Your Adventure:

1. Take photos of the names of restaurants, attractions, and lodging. If you ever return there or someone else wants suggestions, you will have a record of where you went.
2. Always get a card from your hotel upon arrival and keep it with you at all times. If you get lost while exploring, you have the address to give to a taxi or ask for directions. Even if it's in a different language, the card will get you back safely.
3. Experts say you will recover from jet lag quicker upon arrival if you get your bare feet in the grass or sand, spend time in sunlight, and watch the sunset. I plan to test this out on my next long trip!
4. Plan on one day to recover from each hour of time zone change. Jet lag is more severe flying east than west.
5. Don't keep all valuables in one place; divide them up.
6. Don't be in Tourist Lala-land and let your guard down, assuming a place is safe. Research what areas to avoid and ask your local host what precautions to take. Don't stay out too late.
7. Take an extra credit card or ATM card as backup. Sometimes credit card companies lock the use of your card if they see it's

being used somewhere else, so having a second card on hand will be very helpful.

8. In my opinion, the best part of a country is not its mountains or tourist attractions. It's the people, people, people! Trains, buses, bed and breakfasts, local markets, and cafes are great places to meet and talk with locals and other travelers.
9. Take copies of your family photo or be ready to show them on your phone. You can bring small gifts that represent your country to give to those you meet. Something with spiritual content is a great way to share your greatest treasure, your faith in Jesus!

Acknowledgements

First and foremost, I can't express enough gratitude to the Great Adventurer, the One who brought something extraordinary into my ordinary, self-protective life. He gently led me out of my safe little world and made joining in His adventure irresistible. Thanks to His transforming power, I can reach to the skies.

Thanks to my sacrificial and supportive husband, Peter, who participates in many of my crazy ideas and ends up enjoying them. While Jesus is my never-changing solid foundation, you are the person who is always there for me. This book may not have happened without your help and encouragement.

Many thanks to Maggie Bruehl, who once again joined forces with me as my editor-friend. Your excellent skills and suggestions took these stories a few notches higher. Lori Roeleveld and Rachel Streich were also a great help in smoothing out rough edges.

Much appreciation to our generous team of ministry partners, who have walked alongside us through these adventures and shown us the faithfulness of God. Your partnership has eternally impacted us and those we have ministered to.

Thanks to my faithful online prayer team, who prayed for this book each step of the way and gave valuable input and encouragement that helped make it what it is.

Thank you, my Word Weavers friends. You have given me an enjoyable place to belong, have spurred me on, and have refined my writing skills.

Much appreciation to the National Tapestry and Sonshine Award judges, who granted this book awards even before it was completed.

And last but not least, thank you, my dear reader, for taking the time to read these stories I poured myself into for countless hours. Knowing you have read them and, I pray, have been inspired to seek God and His plan for your life, makes it all worthwhile.

About Nancy Beverly

Little did this cautious, small-town girl know the adventures that lay ahead when she asked Jesus to come into her life.

Since then, Nancy has traveled to 31 countries and she's not done yet. She saw penguins in Africa, kangaroos in Australia, sunsets in Malaysia, and Big Ben in London. She was hugged by an elephant in Thailand and danced with locals in Turkey. Nancy knows what it's like to struggle at times with doubts and despair, and has dealt with self-criticism, heartache, and loss. These things have made her more human and a better writer and friend.

Her most meaningful adventure has been knowing the God of the universe and seeing Him do amazing things only He could do. This includes Jesus changing people's lives all over the world.

Nancy also loves traveling, being creative, bike riding, jazzercise, and gardening. She loves meeting new people and discovering each one's unique journey. There's always time for talking with her husband and anything with her four adult children and seven grandchildren.

Check out her website! **nancybeverlyauthor.com**

Also by Nancy Beverly

If you enjoyed *Discover Your Great Adventure,* you will love *Tire Tracks*!

We invite you to walk alongside Nancy as she brings to life her journey of faith over the years. Her collection of easy-to-read short stories narrates how God unmistakably showed up for big things, like her close call with a speeding truck, and small things, like a shower curtain. This interactive book will inspire you to draw closer to the totally trustworthy God.

Available for purchase on Amazon.com by scanning the QR code below.

Also Available in Simplified Chinese

Available for purchase on Amazon.com by scanning the QR code below.

Made in the USA
Coppell, TX
19 January 2026